# Real Questions, Real Answers

## Focusing Teacher Leadership on School Improvement

JOHN H. CLARKE • STEPHEN D. SANBORN • JUDITH A. AIKEN
NANCY A. CORNELL • JANE BRIODY GOODMAN • KARIN K. HESS

Association for Supervision and Curriculum Development
Alexandria, Virginia USA

Association for Supervision and Curriculum Development
1250 N. Pitt Street • Alexandria, Virginia 22314-1453 USA
Telephone: 1-800-933-2723 or 703-549-9110 • Fax: 703-299-8631
Web site: http://www.ascd.org • E-mail: member@ascd.org

Gene R. Carter, *Executive Director*
Michelle Terry, *Assistant Executive Director, Program Development*
Nancy Modrak, *Director, Publishing*
John O'Neil, *Acquisitions Editor*
Mark Goldberg, *Development Editor*
Julie Houtz, *Managing Editor of Books*
Jo Ann Irick Jones, *Senior Associate Editor*
Kathleen Larson Florio, *Copy Editor*
Deborah Whitley, *Proofreader*
Gary Bloom, *Director, Editorial, Design, and Production Services*
Karen Monaco, *Senior Designer*
Tracey A. Smith, *Production Manager*
Dina Murray, *Production Assistant*
Valerie Sprague, *Desktop Publisher*

Printed in the United States of America.

s2/98

ASCD Stock No.: 198007
ASCD member price: $11.95; nonmember price: $14.95

**Library of Congress Cataloging-in-Publication Data**
Real questions, real answers : focusing teacher leadership on school
    improvement / John H. Clarke . . . [et al.].
        p.    cm.
    Includes bibliographical references.
    ISBN 0-87120-293-X (pbk.)
    1. School improvement programs—Vermont—Case studies.   2. School
management and organization—Vermont—Case Studies.   3. Problem-
solving—Vermont—Case studies.   4. Group work in education—
Vermont—Case studies.   I. Clarke, John H.,   1943–
LB2822.83.V5R43     1998
371.2'009743—dc21                                        97-33941
                                                           CIP

# REAL QUESTIONS, REAL ANSWERS: FOCUSING TEACHER LEADERSHIP ON SCHOOL IMPROVEMENT

# PREFACE:

# GATHERING ENERGY FOR

# SCHOOL DEVELOPMENT

JOHN H. CLARKE

W ith the school year ending, nearly 100 teachers from Essex Junction, Vermont, gathered in the meeting room of a local inn to share the final results of their problem-based school development (PBSD) inquiries. Some carried examples of student work they would use to illustrate their results. Others carried cardboard boxes or loose-leaf binders, portfolios of materials developed by their teams. Each had worked with a team of 2 to 25 other teachers throughout the year to investigate and solve a problem related to teaching and learning in the district schools. Most were enrolled in a university program that granted credit for their PBSD work, but such enrollment was not mandatory for their participation on a team.

After three consecutive years of problem solving in teams, the Essex Junction teachers had grown accustomed to working independently in behalf of an emerging school development agenda and their own need for professional development. For their final presentations, each team was prepared to define the problem situation they had faced in the fall, review what they had learned about the problem, describe effects of the solutions they had developed through field testing, and recommend to the district specific steps for continuing work on the problem. In addition, each teacher had written an individual summary to demonstrate continuing growth within professional development plans required for relicensure in Vermont.

Problem-based school development is a process that gathers the energy and talent of a school faculty and focuses it on specific and immediate problems that come up during a school reform effort. Conducted over several years, simultaneous team investigations of problems in teaching and learning constitute a method for linking school development to professional development and creating a professional community capable of sustaining long-term educational reform.

At the year-end gathering in Essex Junction, the elementary teams reported first. One team had spent the year developing a report card format that would encourage parents to play a greater role in their child's growth. A 1st grade teacher presented her part of the team's report:

> We sought and found a variety of report cards from other schools as well as read professional articles on the subject. The challenge was how to report to parents what we are teaching their children in a manner that reflects what we teach and assess. This has pushed—enabled—us to finally do what for years we had only dreamed.

Teachers from the upper grades listened attentively, wondering, perhaps, how much room their own report cards create for parent involvement.

A primary grade team then described the teaching units they had developed to begin integrating computer technology in classroom work. During the inquiry phase of their work, they had discovered that they would have to explore thematic curriculum to make the best use of available software. Because computers work best with one or two students learning together, they found themselves moving away from a whole-class to a project-based format. With their students working independently on computers, they then had to develop a performance-based assessment plan that allowed for differences among student projects. The size of their "problem" had expanded over the year, as had the complexity of their solutions.

One teacher noted,

I learned an immense amount about our eight-week unit topic called "structures"—concepts surrounding bridges, towers, tunnels, and architectural design—that I never knew and that is not normally taught at the primary level.

Another team member added,

Our students are integrating research into their coursework using computers. They are very comfortable using computers to organize themselves. . . . They can get a professional-looking product done much sooner.

High school science teachers in the room, who had already decided their next problem would be computer integration, gained from the primary teams an enlarged view of the problem they would face in the year to come. Would they also have to focus on themes to integrate technology? Would they settle on a project-based format? What would happen to their grading system? The primary team's presentation—and its implication for situations that other teachers were facing—made clear that what appear to be simple adaptations in teaching can slowly force a whole system to change.

Several middle school teams had created and field-tested interdisciplinary units, with the intent of increasing student involvement in classroom work. Hoping to extend the success of their previous year's work, one group had included the language teachers in an expanded team. A 6th grade teacher described the process:

Our entire team confronted new information as we welcomed foreign language teachers into our family of core 6th grade team members. I enjoyed working on our various thematic units involving Spanish and French teachers as we planned and executed our curriculum. Between the workshops we attended, courses we studied, and conferences we traveled to, we created a product that was challenging to our students and ourselves.

The experience of the team of teachers and all their students learning new material at the same time had challenged and excited the whole middle school.

In another middle school team, physical education and health teachers had decided to move away from purely competitive activities toward new, noncompetitive challenges for students in their physical education classes. As one teacher described it,

> The Project Adventure and Challenge by Choice materials were all totally new to me. We relied on information from three workshops, other area professionals who had implemented similar programs, as well as seven books on cooperative games and group initiatives. We encountered no programs organized like ours—in that ours was an entire year of "adventure" and not a single unit.

Although unplanned at the outset, the confluence of interdisciplinary academic teams and the P.E.-health team's emphasis on Project Adventure has since led many other teachers in the middle school toward a new interest in cooperative learning.

Seven high school teams had begun the year without a unifying focus. Instead, three of the teams had struggled with teaching problems related to their own classrooms. An English-social studies team, for example, had decided to experiment with designing interdisciplinary units. To fuse two different subjects, the team had reorganized their merged classes to study six chronologically arranged themes in American culture. A team member described the evolution of the coursework:

> Basically, students are answering questions for themselves that relate to our themes. We weren't aware that these questions existed until we taught the course for a while and repeatedly came back to them. The class itself is now a synthesis. Music, literature, art, and technology are used to present information both by us and by our students.

A merger of two disciplines had opened the door to additional subjects. During the next round of problem-based school development, a new interdisciplinary team would take this innovation one step further, creating a computer-based multimedia library of art, artifacts, and primary materials for all students and teachers to use in making interdisciplinary presentations.

What sense can we make of this wild diversity? None of the team presentations represent enactment of a large-scale district plan. No team was told what problem to confront. Still, among projects carried out in five separate schools, a remarkable confluence had occurred:

- All the teams shifted classroom emphasis from knowledge retention toward student performance.
- All found ways to accommodate individual differences and engage students in independent learning.
- Most crossed the subject boundaries in search of meaningful ways to organize learning for students.
- Most attempted to use technology as a way to accommodate increasingly complex teaching plans.
- Many experimented with alternative assessment as a way to engage multiple intelligences and link content learning to student performance.

As a collective whole, the Essex Junction teams had developed a comprehensive set of adaptations to other changes occurring in their community, in the state, and in educational reform in the United States. The changes they proposed created a new set of internal tensions that fresh teams would have to resolve in the year to come. The proposed changes also stretched the boundaries of existing policy, forcing governing boards to rethink the rules that restrict school growth.

The appearance of interconnectedness among many separate teams is more than good luck. As individuals succeed with small explorations, a shared vision of learning begins to evolve within a PBSD team. The simultaneous work of many teams, carried out over time, evolves gradually into a shared vision of how a school curriculum should work. As teams put connected improvements in place, systems and procedures slowly adapt to fit—by instituting new class schedules, department structures, and grading practices, for example—taking forms that allow further growth to continue. Just as individual effort brings eventual cohesion to team problem solving, the many solutions that school-based teams create to solve specific problems also tend to connect, folding together to suggest a larger, more comprehensive sense of how the schools work together as interacting parts of one dynamic system.

Problem-based school development is essentially a process of professional inquiry—an intellectual and social experience for teachers—rather than a school governance strategy. Gathering new information about a problem from background and action research prevents a team from becoming just one more committee that sits together to hash out a recommendation based on what the members already happen to know. In PBSD, a team of individuals forms to solve a problem they are facing separately. They organize their work around questions they generate about the problem situation (see fig. i.1). They search for new information—from the library, living sources, communication networks, and local field tests—to gain a sense of what might work as part of a solution. They organize local inquiry projects in their own school. They report their findings to other teams and their own faculty at the end of a year.

## FIGURE i.1.
## Problem-Based School Development

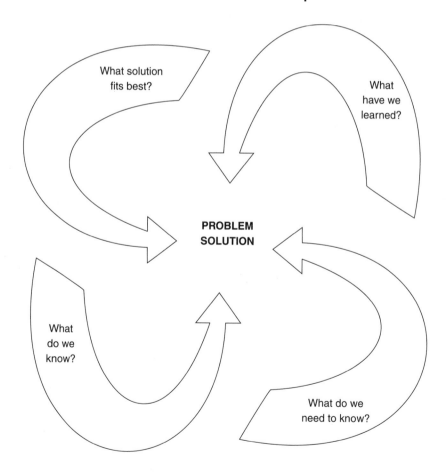

What solution fits best?

What have we learned?

PROBLEM SOLUTION

What do we know?

What do we need to know?

The drive to develop and test solutions to real problems makes PBSD an authentic learning experience, managed by independent teams of teachers who teach themselves by working together.

In Vermont, problem-based school development supports decentralized reform initiatives. The *Vermont Framework of Standards and Learning Opportunities* provides general guidelines for teachers to use in designing curriculum for their own schools. At a similar level of generality, the *Standards for Vermont Educators* outlines five broad goals teachers use to develop yearly individual professional development plans for relicensure, in concert with local relicensing boards made up of teachers, administrators, and community members. Both the curriculum standards and the teacher relicensing standards create a climate that favors teacher-led reform, channeling professional energy toward general goals established for all students and teachers.

Problem-based school development evolved during more than 10 years of partnership between Vermont schools and the University of Vermont—aiming to improve learning for *all* studens. Problem-Based School Development Institutes, or School Development Institutes (SDIs), are yearlong courses—but not in the traditional sense. They offer graduate credits for teacher-led school development initiatives across the state, involving schools with faculties ranging in number from 25 to 135. Schools and the university have formed Professional Development Schools in seven local secondary schools to serve as the administrative centers for the SDIs. In addition, the Professional Development Schools are sites where graduate students in education serve as interns and complete their requirements for a master's degree and a license to teach while working on the forward edge of school change.

Although the process of school development described in this book has emerged from a long-term relationship between schools and the university, it has also begun to take hold in Vermont schools that have no such relationship. This book reflects the belief that problem-based school development may prove useful in school change whether or not schools and a university have established a special relationship for graduate credits, graduate degrees, and resource sharing in behalf of improved learning.

Problem-based school development aims to support the emergence of a learning community in a public school setting, a flexible organization that generates information and uses that information to change itself. PBSD derives its energy from the individual initiative that team members bring to their vision of the problem situation. Individuals join a team because they are concerned about some aspect of their work with students. As team members, these individuals conduct their own research for the group, present their findings, propose and field-test "solutions," and work politically to institute specific changes. Teams, on the other hand, struggle together to fit individuals' contributions into an evolving sense of what the problem situation demands. As the school year goes on, the problem situation changes, altered both by the unpredictable influence of outside forces and by the explicit efforts of the team to make a positive difference in the situation. Focusing a team of teachers on specific problems in teaching and learning concentrates professional energy on the areas that make a difference in the life of any school.

Problem-based school development works from the "bottom" of the educational system, among teachers and their students. PBSD begins with the natural desire of adult professionals to take control of the situations they face on a daily basis; it then organizes that energy to support systemwide change.

After this Preface and Chapter 1 on the mechanics of problem-based school development, the remaining chapters of this book focus on the dynamics of PBSD from various perspectives within the school organization. When change is being driven from the bottom rather than the top, teachers as well as school and district administrators need to adapt their own leadership roles to support the growth of a self-directed learning community. Stories from five school districts in Vermont where PBSD is being tested and refined make up the core of this book, accompanied by our thoughts on the promise of teacher-led teams in school improvement. We believe that any school district can use our experience and form problem-based learning teams to carry out reform where it counts the most—in school programs that help students learn.

# 1

# HOW PROBLEM-BASED SCHOOL DEVELOPMENT WORKS

JOHN H. CLARKE AND STEPHEN D. SANBORN

I n the spring of 1993 two teachers from the alternative program at Essex High School in Essex Junction, Vermont,
brought a problem to a meeting of three school and district
administrators. The teachers had observed more and more
students from the high school and the alternative program—the
Alternative Center for Education (ACE)—reaching the age of 17 or
18 with a discouragingly small number of credits toward graduation. These students had not been successful in their first two or
three years of high school. Some had failed courses or had missed
too many classes to earn credit. Others had encountered personal
problems that distracted them from school. The difference between
these students and those who just drop out was that these students
had come to recognize the value of a high school diploma and
wanted to earn one.

As their age-mates graduated, these students had only two options: they could choose to stay at the high school or in the ACE
program for an additional two or three years to complete required
credits, or they could drop out of school and hope to get a GED
certificate later. Neither of these choices looked good to the stu-

dents involved, to the teachers from ACE, or to the high school teachers.

The five educators meeting for the first time that day in Essex agreed that the chances of these students succeeding in the existing system were minimal, but none had an acceptable answer to the question of how to help the students graduate. After discussing the need for alternative systems, the five teachers and administrators decided to form a team and join the district's Problem-Based School Development Institute, becoming one of 15 teams working on various problems for the high school that year.

## Organizing to Solve Ill-Defined Problems

Like the issue of older students without enough credits for graduation, the problems that come up in school development tend to be "ill-defined"; that is, the problems that really make a difference in school development are too complex for easy answers. Some ill-defined problems have multiple causes. For example, students who reach the age of 18 without meeting graduation requirements have different educational histories, defying a singular solution for all. Simply letting all 18-year-olds graduate without sufficient credits would offend virtually all other teachers and students, and letting them drop out would raise the ire of parents, social service agencies, and the school board.

Because problems in learning and teaching are often complex, ill-defined, and interconnected, problem-based school development teams work on one problem situation for a full school year. Ill-defined problems put pressure on team members to develop a deep knowledge of the subject before they begin to consider solutions. They examine the multiple origins of the problem situation and test many different kinds of solutions. Sharing individual discoveries, initiating small classroom experiments, reviewing recent research, and trying to make sense of a constantly shifting situation may lead a team in unpredictable directions. Bill Stepien and his colleagues at the Illinois Mathematics and Science Institute (Stepien, Gallagher, and Workman 1993) studied ill-defined problems in some detail. Their paraphrased observations follow:

- More knowledge than is initially available will be needed (a) to understand what is occurring and (b) to decide what actions are required for resolution.
- Because every problem and problem solver is unique, there is no absolutely right way or fixed formula for conducting an investigation.
- As new information is obtained, the problem changes.
- You can never be sure you have made the right decision because important information is lacking, [and] data or values may be in conflict; but decisions have to be made.

Team members working through an ill-defined problem gain respect for the volume of knowledge related to any problem situation and also recognize the element of risk that accompanies any solution. Nevertheless, each school development team aims to assemble within a year a comprehensive solution to the problem it has selected.

In problem-based school development the team itself takes on much of the work of the "teacher/facilitator/tutor." Each team must develop its own organization, schedule, resource base, and project outcome. The team itself must learn to keep the process moving, to probe and challenge, and to keep the members usefully engaged. Under the structure developed in Vermont, course coordinators from the University of Vermont call all the teams from an institute together four times during the year to report on their progress and inform the rest of the faculty about possible solutions, but the team itself controls its own process. Although the substance of a school problem and its solutions remain in the forefront, team members must also be continuously aware of their place in the process.

Simultaneous attention to content and process is a requirement for any teacher. In a team of peers, however, the absence of set roles makes this more difficult. Individual team members must establish and then adapt their own roles continuously, helping others see how they connect to the team and to the problem-solving process. In problem-based school development, team members go public with what they have learned at regular intervals, struggling to assemble a coherent presentation with others who have learned differently. Given the public nature of PBSD, team members pay as much attention to strategy in their approach as to the substance of the problem itself.

Problem-based school development relies on a set of questions team members can ask, with appropriate adaptation, as they struggle to understand a problem in depth and then to search widely for the solution that fits best and costs least:

- *What is happening?* Teams describe the problem situation in enough detail to activate what the group already knows about the problem.
- *What do we need to know?* Teams generate questions about the situation and figure out how those questions can be answered.
- *What have we learned?* Teams assemble new information from background and action research in a way that reveals how the problem has come into being, creating a model of the specific problem.
- *What solutions fit the model?* Teams propose a "best-fit" solution and field-test some of its parts; they use all available information to propose a comprehensive solution to guide development during the following year.

The search for new information—from libraries, living sources, communication networks, and local field tests—makes problem-based school development an authentic learning experience, managed by independent teams of teachers.

Individuals on a team take on different tasks in both research and development—to find information and to make events happen—as well as to help the whole team see how specific elements support the emergence of a general solution. The whole team takes responsibility not only for testing and refining specific solutions, but also for publicly presenting its findings and fitting its general solution into the ongoing life of the school.

Letting a team confront a problem situation from the personal perspective of team members, then work through channels of inquiry that appear only after a team is in motion creates unnerving vacillations in team process—as well as sudden creative insight. The challenges of team problem solving—including dead ends, team breakdowns, and periods of debilitating confusion—make the process itself as interesting to teachers as the volumes of information and experience they generate.

# Four Phases of Inquiry

Figure 1.1 illustrates the four phases of problem-based school development in terms of teamwork over a full school year. In June, teams gather to describe their situation, define their problems, and begin planning their work. From July through December, teams conduct both action research and background research on their problem and start to explore solutions. In January each team reports the initial findings from its research and discusses possible best-fit solutions with other teams. From January through May, teams test solutions that look promising, make adjustments, and assess results. In May, each team produces a team report explaining and documenting a best-fit solution for its school, making its report available to other teachers. In Vermont, the university and the Association for Supervision and Curriculum Development (ASCD) have set up a home page on the Internet that provides access to reports from various schools. In addition, individual team members who are seeking university credit summarize their work for the year in a report that gets a university grade. All team members reflect on their own personal and professional growth for their professional development plans.

The four questions that organize a school development team appear to be neat and linear—but our experience tells us that PBSD is far from a neat, linear process. Teams often jump toward solutions without clearly defining the problem or doing adequate research. Teams discover, sometimes after months of work, that what originally appeared to be a problem that needed fixing was not the real problem at all. Teams test promising solutions and then throw them out—only to start again with a fresh view of the situation. They test solutions and come up with new information that leads them in completely unexpected directions. Teams often end a cycle recognizing a whole set of new problems that emerged from their inquiry, then re-form to work another year on newly apparent problems. The four flexible questions allow teams to understand where they are at any moment and to correct the path of their inquiry to fit their changing sense of the problem situation.

## FIGURE 1.1
## Four Phases of Problem-Based School Development

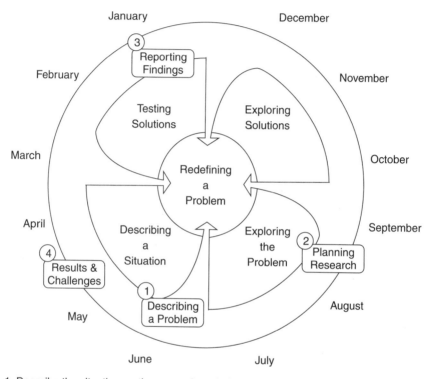

1. Describe the situation: gather group knowledge, generate questions, and identify resources.
2. Investigate the problem: conduct background research, locate examples of potential solutions, and schedule action.
3. Report findings from exploration and propose a best-fit solution for field-testing.
4. Report conclusions and make recommendations.

## Phase 1: What Is the Problem Situation? What Is Happening?

At the beginning of a cycle, teams in an institute gather to review the process of problem-based school development and to clarify the problem they have set out to solve. Individuals in any single team may have the same general problem in view and still see the situation quite differently. When a team first meets, each individual describes the situation from his or her perspective and analyzes why the problem is occurring. Figure 1.2 shows an example of this description and analysis, presented in typical written format, from one of the members of the ACE team mentioned at the start of this chapter. In the ACE team, individuals with different roles tended to focus on different parts of the problem:

*First ACE teacher:* These students "come to life" academically only after a period of sometimes painful experiences at home and in school.

*Second ACE teacher:* Most of them lost ground in credits during their first two years of high school, when they failed to see any connection between their classes and their lives outside of school.

*The principal:* Students are more likely to lose credits in the core academic areas than in applied or hands-on areas of the curriculum.

*The special education coordinator:* Like many students in special education, these students do not learn in one uniform way; each has developed a different style and a different set of personal goals.

*The curriculum coordinator:* The school board has settled on academic credits as the determining standard for graduation, but they are also talking about "raising standards" for all students.

The team's final recommendation has to accommodate each individual's perspective on the problem. Otherwise the solution the team finally develops may fail to work or to be accepted by the community-at-large.

Fusing their separate perspectives, the team members struggle to fashion a comprehensive, though still provisional, statement of the problem. For the ACE team, the problem statement connected the plight of older students who have few credits to policies guaranteeing a certain standard of education for all students:

*Problem Statement:* A significant number of high school students discover late in their careers that their future depends on a high school diploma, a critically important discovery occurring too late to allow them to attain their goals. The

7

high school, on the other hand, relies on a credit system based on grades and seat time to represent "high standards" for all students, including those for whom seat time and grades are not a good measure of performance. The community-at-large has not begun to think of standards in any other terms but credits and grades. As long as credits and grades are the only acceptable evidence of achievement, a significant number of able and committed students will leave school without a diploma, creating a number of problems for the larger community.

The problem statement provides a launching point for team investigation, as well as a checkpoint for solutions proposed during the year.

### FIGURE 1.2.
### Problem Description and Analysis
#### (Derived from Individual Logs)

Team name:
Team members:

#### Problem description: What's happening?
Peter and Lars described students from ACE and the high school who have reached the age of 17 or 18 without the number of credits that would make graduation feasible. As these students see their friends graduate, they have only two choices: they can stay at ACE or the high school for another two or three years to complete the required credits, or they can drop out now and hope to get a GED certificate later. Even if they stay on in school for another semester or two, most choose to leave school rather than suffer increasing humiliation as they reach 20 or 21. Steve doesn't think the school board will agree to adjust credit requirements. Neither will high school teachers.

#### Problem analysis: Why is it happening?
- Most of these students run into trouble in the middle school or during their first year at the high school.
- Some fail a number of courses required for graduation, rather than electives.
- Others miss too many classes to qualify for credit.
- Individuals encounter any number of personal problems as they enter high school, such as drugs, family break-up, scrapes with the law, pregnancy, or some unique combination of distractions.
- These students do realize through experience that they need an education.

## Phase 2: What Do We Need to Know?

With a first statement of the problem in hand, teams generate questions they will need to answer in order to propose a workable solution. The first list of questions gives a team a starting point, but the list typically grows longer as the team becomes familiar with available resources. The ACE team generated some questions that could be answered by a search of school records, other questions that would require a search of the literature on graduation requirements, and still others that would require action research with real students at the high school:

- Who are these students? Gender? Background? Educational history?
- How do they get into this situation?
- What do they believe? Goals? Resentments?
- What alternatives to credits and grades exist? Are they valid?
- Has anybody created a list of standards for graduation?
- How do you measure achievement without grades and seat time?
- How do educators make graduation standards acceptable?
- What alternative delivery systems are required?
- Do students respond well to alternative delivery systems?
- What does an alternative system cost?

Each of the questions generated at this point can be answered using information from a variety of different resources—books, films, articles, consultants, conferences, Internet contacts, or school visits. Each source of information is associated with a cost in either time or money. Some costs are low, such as those associated with checking library articles and school records, and others, such as conference travel, are high. The team uses its question list to prepare a preliminary inquiry plan that fits the problem as well as the budget. Figure 1.3 shows the ACE team's preliminary inquiry plan.

After agreeing that they were looking at the same problem but needed more information about solutions, the ACE team members decided to meet every other week for two hours starting in mid-September. At the first September meeting they would organize the research process and decide how the team would use available resources to support their inquiry. This would involve a number of practical considerations: How many questions require the work of

9

the whole team? How many can one team member answer? How can we locate the best answers with the funds we have available?

**FIGURE 1.3**
**Preliminary Inquiry Plan**
**(Due to Coordinator in Early Fall)**

| Inquiry Initiative: Activity | By Whom? | When? | Costs |
|---|---|---|---|
| Find out who is included in this and develop a profile for the whole group. | Armando | mid-October | time |
| Do other schools in this area have the same problem? Make calls to similar schools. | Steve | mid-October | time |
| Search the Internet for possible alternatives. | Lars | November | time |
| Discuss the problem with students, looking for workable ideas. | Peter | November | time |
| Visit Littleton High School. | Armando, Lars | December | $1,250 |
| Visit University Heights H.S. | Peter | January | $625 |
| Study findings and present to the other teams. | All | January | |

**Plan for team meetings:**
We will meet as a team every other week on Wednesdays after school for two hours, starting after school opens in September. The first meeting will be used to refine the questions and plan the research process. By first meeting, we should have good estimates of our costs.

After assessing the problem situation, the ACE team decided to begin research on a possible solution—substituting standards-based graduation requirements for Carnegie units for some high school students. The team knew of two high schools in the United States that were experimenting with new models, and they decided to send team members to each of these schools to gather information that might be helpful. One team member traveled to Littleton,

Colorado, to research the standards-based curriculum there. Another collected examples of performance-based testing from various schools, including University Heights High School in New York. Another began working with the school board to test its willingness to adopt any alternative system. Other team members gathered information from ERIC searches and started researching the *Vermont Framework of Standards and Learning Opportunities* to see how it might fit the local situation.

Team members who gather information from any source report their findings back to the team, a practice that continually shapes the team's sense of the problem and also begins to narrow the field of possible solutions. Seldom does a team discover answers that can be plugged into a solution without adaptation. In the case of the ACE team, for example, team members found that Vermont's *Framework* had 133 standards, few with reliable measures. The Littleton program had 22 standards, each with a discrete set of measures; and the University Heights program had only 7 standards, measured by a consensus process among teachers and parents, rather than by specific rubrics and benchmarks. The Littleton program was developed for three large schools—and it eventually lost the backing of its board. The University Heights program worked well for a few hundred students in a system serving many thousands, so widespread acceptability was less a concern. A local team must take information such as the ACE team's findings and construct a model of the problem in its own school in a way that suggests a range of solutions that fit the local situation.

## Phase 3: What Have We Learned?

At the midyear meeting in January all teams involved in the School Development Institute describe what they have learned from their research. After several months of exploration, teams usually have narrowed the range of possibilities and weighed the costs and benefits of each. They have established a way of looking at the problem that supports the solutions they want to test—they have created a model of the problem. In many cases, teams at the midpoint have already designed and field-tested components of the proposed solutions. In reporting their findings to other teams, they create a level of general awareness that brings them useful feedback during the last few months of their project.

Figure 1.4 shows the format the ACE team used in its midterm presentation to summarize the findings. After describing its findings, bolstered by stories from New York and Colorado, the ACE team reported on its decision to pilot an outcome-based assessment system and a standards-driven curriculum and assessment system with students from ACE who might choose to participate. The idea of bypassing Carnegie credits created considerable discussion at the school in the following weeks. Some teachers supported the idea, but many others felt threatened by the impact that it might have on their own classes. Others noticed the confluence between the idea of a standards-driven diploma and similar ideas being developed at the same time: writing portfolios in the English department, a pre-test for 9th grade students in science, and year-end "performances" for students in the social studies department to present to parents. Such simultaneous development of several projects in one school allows creative interplay among projects and also raises the kinds of questions a whole school must answer to promote schoolwide change.

## Phase 4: What Solutions Fit?

In the final phase of problem-based school development, teams complete their field tests, document the effects they have seen in student learning, and prepare their final recommendations for the year-end meeting of all the teams. Team reports include a description of the problem situation, a review of the research they conducted to understand the problem and locate solutions, materials developed for field testing, and results observed in student work. In Vermont, individuals complete a personal reflection for their professional portfolios and, if they are enrolled in the university course, for a university grade. Figure 1.5 outlines the university course requirements.

From January to May the ACE team continued to meet on a regular basis, and by May they had designed a new curriculum around the four "vital results" found in the *Vermont Framework:* (1) communications, (2) reasoning and problem solving, (3) personal development, and (4) social responsibility. The team defined assessment criteria for these vital results in five content areas: language, the social sciences, math, science, and the arts. Team members used many resources to create this curriculum. They placed existing state documents and curriculum documents from the high school at the core of their work, thus avoiding any suggestion of lowering or compromising existing standards for graduation.

**FIGURE 1.4.**
**Midterm Presentation of Initial Findings**

| **Problem Overview:** That our students discover that they need a diploma is exactly what we want. Other schools have created solutions. | |
|---|---|
| **Major findings: What we learned** | **Demonstrations and illustrations** |
| **Background research literature**<br>The Lion's Cave, Direction 2000<br>*Vermont Framework of Standards*<br>Littleton and University Heights High Schools | Graduation requirements<br>State guidelines<br>Portfolio processes |
| **Media**<br>Conference on Integration (ASCD)<br>*Reporting Student Progress* (ASCD) | Videos on program design<br>Standards-based curriculum |
| **Other teachers**<br>Teachers at Littleton, University Heights, and Champlain Valley Union High Schools | A pile of great ideas<br>and materials |
| **Bibliography of Published Sources** | (See attached list) |
| **Proposed field tests:** Next team steps toward a best-fit solution.<br>After observing schools in Colorado, New York, and Hinesburg, we have decided to develop and test parts of a standards-driven curriculum and assessment system for students older than 18. We will use our existing curriculum at the high school with the Vermont Framework to guide our work. We will propose changing graduation requirements from Carnegie units to student demonstration of selected standards. We will gather examples from our work to back up the proposal we develop for the board. | |

During a year of research and development, the ACE curriculum grew from a concept into a document that would guide learning for those students who might choose an alternative route to graduation. To graduate, each student would have to exhibit competencies for each of the defined standards. The student's motivation would determine the length of this process. Seat time and Carnegie units no longer stood as obstacles to older students moti-

## FIGURE 1.5.
## Course Requirements for School Development Institute

**Team Responsibilities:** (75% of individual grade)

The final report should include information from all four phases of problem solving in a coherent presentation for the course instructor and community of educators.

I.  Definition of the problem: Description and analysis of the problem situation

II.  Inquiry plan: What we needed to know
    Research questions about the problem and solutions
    Resources for each question
    Plan for gathering information from resources
    Schedule of major events

III.  Findings: How does this problem happen? How can we solve it?
    Summary of research findings
    A model (explanation) of the problem
    Alternative solutions explored by the team
    Proposal for a best-fit solution

IV.  Results and recommendations: What worked? What will work?
    What did we accomplish?
    What did we learn?
    What do we propose for the future?
    A list of references consulted (books, articles, and people)

V.  Appendix
    Materials developed by the team to solve the problem
    Evidence of results (artifacts from student work, etc.)

Teams should present their reports to their own school community on one occasion and consider preparing a disk for Web publication.

**Individual Responsibilities:** (25% of individual grade)

| A professional summary: (final report) | Problem log: (ongoing) |
|---|---|
| Content knowledge, professional knowledge, colleagueship, and advocacy | A problem log describing individual inquiry |

The team report and professional summary should be submitted to the course instructor via the School Development Institute coordinators.

vated to graduate with their peers, and high standards would not be compromised.

After completing the standards-based curriculum, the ACE team faced two more challenges: acceptance by the rest of the school staff and by the school board. Would teachers still be concerned about this change? Would the school board approve a policy change in graduation requirements?

First, the team presented the final curriculum to other teams in the School Development Institute. After having several months to think about and discuss the concept as an alternative to traditional graduation, most teachers supported the work of the ACE team. The high school staff presented little opposition. To address the second challenge, the director of curriculum presented the team proposal to the school board, which gave permission for the ACE standards-based graduation program to proceed as a pilot project during the following year.

As in many problem-based school development projects, however, the ACE team ended the year's work by identifying a new and even more challenging problem. Now that the ACE curriculum had identified standards for graduation, what evidence would be acceptable to show competency in each of these standards, and who would judge the evidence? A new problem and a new year— the cycle continues and the school gradually changes to meet the emerging needs of its students.

## Resources from a School-University Partnership

The process of problem-based school development described here emerged from the partnerships between the University of Vermont and schools across the state working on school reform. The examples in this and the following chapters come from Vermont's Professional Development Schools, where school and university teachers have joined together to improve learning for all students (Clarke et al. 1995). Each Professional Development School, housed within a local secondary school, supports a full-year teacher preparation program for 6 to 15 graduate student interns, including both coursework and practicums, as well as a PBSD Institute. Interns working to earn a license to teach often provide important research support for school development teams. Fiscal support comes from a portion of the course tuitions, which are paid to the university by the school district via the school's professional development budget. After subtracting a set fee, the university returns the remainder of the tuition funds to the local partnership, to be split between instructional costs (a university "course coordinator") and the school development teams. Some funding may also be provided for independent study by individuals.

The University of Vermont's tuition rate has provided for team funding at the rate of about $250 per person—or $1,250 for a five-person team. Some districts augment team funds with additional money from external grants. Teams allocate their funds to research and development as they see fit. Most team members in the Vermont program choose to enroll in the yearlong graduate course—the PBSD Institute; teachers who join a team without enrolling in the course do not earn funding for their team, but they do participate in all team activities. Tuition-derived funding has both supported and legitimized the problem-based research and development process, empowering teams to significantly change their schools.

Conducted as a university course, a School Development Institute must meet the criteria set by both school and university for graduate-level study. In a professional field such as education, this means that teams must explore a body of knowledge beyond their own experience and assemble that knowledge into a synthesis that relates uniquely to their professional situation. Obviously, a school district could do problem-based school development without a partnership. The Vermont experience has depended on such a partnership, and we argue strongly for combining school and university resources. In either case, professional education requires that participants acquire new information, put it to work, evaluate the results they achieve, and competently report what they have learned from both research and development. Each of the four phases of problem-based school development helps fulfill one of these requirements. Course coordinators from the university use the rubric shown in Figure 1.6 to assign a grade to team members enrolled for credit.

Partnerships between schools and universities are developing rapidly across the country, but they are not yet typical of school-university relationships (Darling-Hammond 1994). In fact, relationships between schools and universities are often strained as a result of turf struggles, cultural differences, arguments over status, and the ancient rift between theory and practice in education. PBSD offers the opportunity to create a positive relationship, as exemplified by the teacher reactions presented in Figure 1.7.

## FIGURE 1.6.
## Assessment Rubric for School Development
## Institute Team Members

The course instructor will use these criteria in developing a grade for individuals in a School Development Team.

| **Team Presentations: (2) (75%)** | No Reference | Some Reference | Complete Treatment |
|---|---|---|---|
| Describes and analyzes a problem | | | |
| Defines a research agenda | | | |
| Gathers new information from a variety of sources: | | | |

    Oral
    Written
    Exploratory action

Defines a working model of the problem

Describes a variety of possible solutions

Tests a unique solution with results

Recommends a future course of action

Artifacts, illustrations, and reference list

Presentation to community of educators

**Individual Portfolio: (25%)**

Summary: Evaluates professional growth:
    Content knowledge
    Professional knowledge
    Colleagueship
    Advocacy

Log:    Describes personal role in the problem-based learning team

**Comments:**

In problem-based school development, teachers from the schools and university become involved in a process of mutual education. University teachers push teams toward existing information that may help them solve the problems they face. School teachers provide university teachers with new information derived from both theory and experience that has been tested in the halls and classrooms of real schools. When PBSD is organized into a graduate course, teachers from both settings become members of the same learning community. They empower each other as members of one profession who have different roles but one purpose: improved learning for all students.

## FIGURE 1.7.
### Essex Junction Teacher Reactions to
### Problem-Based School Development

**Impact**
The kids receive the benefit of what teachers learn.
**Coherence**
Students see that all the teachers are moving in one general direction.
**Utility**
You remember better because you use what you are learning.
**Progress**
One round of learning launches you into the next.
**Results**
The teams produce results that change the way schools work.

**Focusing on the process**

**Time**
Integrating learning with work reduces diffusion of effort.
**Connections**
Nothing is wasted in the translation of new knowledge to new professional practice.
**Cooperation**
Working together carries over into other areas of school life.
**Colleagueship**
Even students recognize that we are working like a family.
**Risk**
The process makes us branch out, doing things we never thought we would do.

# 2

# LINKING ADULT LEARNING

# AND SCHOOL DEVELOPMENT

JUDITH A. AIKEN

T he research seems clear. When teachers are encouraged to engage in self-directed inquiry about their own instructional practices, they create powerful learning environments for themselves and their students. Lieberman (1996) has conducted numerous studies that address the need to create professional learning that "moves away from the traditional inservice mode toward long-term, continuous learning in the context of school and classroom with support of colleagues" (p. 186). If these findings are valid, a critical question remains: Can a school system support the self-directed professional growth of adult learners in a way that also improves student learning throughout a school?

The idea of autonomous learning seems inconsistent, at first glance, with the need for professional development programs or-

*Author's Note:* I would like to thank Linda Berger, Holly Scudder-Chase, Barbara Colf, Elizabeth Nicholson, and Ginny Zahner for the teacher leadership they extend on behalf of student learning and for their support in writing this chapter. Appreciation is also extended to their school principal, Duncan Tingle, and curriculum coordinator, Jude Newman, for their support of this project.

ganized to promote schoolwide change. Adults who have spent many years in a profession have a need to ask their own questions, pursue their own answers, and perhaps consult with others as they make changes in their work. Schools, on the other hand, have a need to reduce the diffusion that results when too many priorities and too little coordination make a hodgepodge of the school day and the curriculum. A large group inservice program in which all teachers receive the same information in order to produce a uniform result reflects administrative concern for broad, unifying goals to the same extent that it violates what we know about how adults learn. What educators in central Vermont came to realize through problem-based school development is the value of viewing professional development as an integral part of teaching, and the importance of constructing school and professional development consistent with the adult need for autonomy in inquiry.

The Central Vermont Region includes four major school districts including the capital city of Montpelier. With the exception of Montpelier, which is a city school district that houses its own elementary, middle, and senior high school, each school district in the surrounding region is made up of three to five towns, each of which supports its own individual elementary school, but shares a middle school and a high school. The Central Vermont Region partnered with the University of Vermont and organized a PBSD Institute. Teachers from the region's 12 elementary, middle, and secondary schools were invited to form teams and to enroll in the yearlong institute. My role as a university faculty member was to help develop the Central Vermont PBSD and to facilitate a number of teams within the institute.

In an attempt to harmonize district and teacher needs, we organized our PBSD Institute around four broad themes or strands: (1) Curriculum and Assessment, (2) Technology, (3) Diversity, and (4) a wildcard strand we called Teachers as Leaders. Unlike the three strands that represented district development priorities, Teachers as Leaders had no preset goal or agenda. We included the Teachers as Leaders option to allow individuals to explore their own concerns about classroom instruction. With time to research and reflect on potential solutions to curricular problems, we hoped that a wildcard team might discover ways to reduce teacher isolation, share expertise, and find emotional support as the members attempted to implement change in their own classrooms (Wildman and Niles 1987).

We disseminated brochures and registration materials to all teachers and administrators in the Central Vermont Region inviting them to form a team and select a strand around which they could build their problem-based team inquiry. More than 80 teachers and administrators assembled on a Monday morning in June to join the institute. At the three-day kick-off, 12 different teams came together to establish a team focus and plan their yearlong team inquiry. Five teachers from the Montpelier Union Elementary School selected the Teachers as Leaders strand, forming their own school-based team that would enable us to see whether problem-based learning could support both adult learning and school development at the same time. The five teachers made up the entire membership of the Teachers as Leaders group.

## Creating a Context for Adult Learning

Like the more goal-specific groups, the Teachers as Leaders team arrived at Montpelier High School at 8:00 a.m. for refreshments, listened to an introduction to the concept of problem-based school development, and went off to their designated classroom to begin work—where I had been assigned to serve as strand coordinator. The brochure had described our strand only as being appropriate for those teachers wanting to understand the concept of "teacher leadership" and how it could contribute to the school restructuring process. Team members would be able to structure their own problem-based inquiry and define activities, experiences, and opportunities for their own professional growth (Central Vermont School Development Institute Consortium 1995). My role was to support them as this developmental process took shape.

Although they had signed up individually, these teachers soon realized that they had come to the institute in search of new opportunities for professional growth and learning, something beyond the talk-and-listen courses they had taken previously. They all had been involved in a number of school restructuring initiatives over the past several years through their work on committees, panels, community forums, and school-based inservice programs. Their professional development records also revealed that each had completed a substantial number of graduate-level college courses, participating in and presenting at state and national conferences. The array of leadership positions they held in the school gave evidence of the professional competence of these teachers: Holly directed the school music program; Linda served as copresident of the teachers union; Elizabeth headed the school's instructional support team; Ginny served as a learning specialist; and Barbara participated as a teacher leader on the school's multi-age, grades 1–3, enrichment team.

Sitting around the table that first morning, the five elementary school teachers talked openly about why they had come to the institute. In addition to searching for new opportunities for professional growth, these teachers were looking for a deeper understanding of their practice and its effect on students, and for support from within their own school to sustain them in their curriculum development work. Holly expressed it this way:

> When I first heard about the institute and read the brochure, I felt without a place. Although I wanted to participate, I had my own idea for school improvement—something I had been thinking about for my students. It just didn't fit in. I just wasn't interested in what they were telling us we had to do. I was looking for something more challenging, something more personal, something for me. Somehow, this strand seemed to fit.

As Linda shared her reasons for joining the problem-based study team, her search for something different also became apparent:

> When I read about the strand, Teachers as Leaders, I knew I wanted to be in it . . . not so much because I was sharing the union presidency, but because of the fatigue with always being on a variety of committees. I didn't want to work on the district strategic plan, because I had been doing that. I wanted to do something that was *my* choice, something that would have more impact on other teachers and our students.

These teachers knew they wanted change. Although they still wanted others to view them as supportive of school development, they were feeling exhausted by their school district's vast array of initiatives and committees. Loss of interest in fragmented professional development activities provided by the district or in traditional university courses was a common complaint in our dialogue that first morning together. The teachers voiced frustration with the lack of impact of those previous efforts on their professional lives and on their students. Paradoxically, districtwide efforts to improve student performance seemed to divert teachers from meaningful work with students.

# Discovering Shared Concerns

The energetic and sometimes conflicting conversation that spanned the first days of the institute helped each teacher in our small group to develop a focus for a yearlong inquiry with an individualistic bent, to gain an expanded awareness of herself as a professional teacher, and to identify the skills and abilities needed to continue as an adult learner. As the dialogue continued, we discovered that a shared *concern for student learning* was leading us inexorably to struggle with a second concern: the fear that *existing school culture* would restrict any progress we might make independently in teaching. As we discussed the problem of the dominant school culture, we were forced again to a third level of concern: that we would have to become *teacher leaders* in order to shift school culture in a direction that would support improved student learning. In short, the problems of student learning that held our attention were driving us to engage the larger school culture and forcing us to consider our leadership roles as well. In a complex situation, problems do not exist in isolation from one another.

Through PBSD, the Teachers as Leaders group found a way to integrate the self-directed investigations of teaching problems with a team investigation of school leadership. The process by which we expanded from our individual concerns with student learning to include school culture and teacher leadership is worth describing in some detail.

## Concern for Students

Each teacher had joined the institute to change a small part of what happened to students in the classroom. As we sat in a small circle with a large blank easel and marker and pen in hand, the teachers articulated their specific reasons for joining the institute.

Ginny was concerned about early literacy instruction and the schools of thought that polarized and fractionalized teachers. She wanted to help rid her school of these "imaginary fences" by developing new ways of working with and supporting teachers as they examined and applied new forms of early literacy instruction.

Holly was concerned that music education needed to be more fully integrated into the curriculum, creating opportunities for more students and teachers to become involved in performances. She wanted to build a more collaborative process through which teachers and students could affect decisions about concert themes and have a role in the performance aspects of the music program.

In her role as facilitator for the school's Instructional Support Team (IST), Elizabeth had come to believe that many of the student learning and classroom management problems brought to the attention of the IST were not being adequately addressed. Recognizing the talents and expertise of many teachers and support personnel in the school, she wanted to find ways for all teachers to access available professional knowledge and experience.

Beginning with a concern for her own classroom, Barbara sought to expand the "enrichment" opportunities for all students in the multi-age (grades 1 through 3) classrooms, which included 5 teachers and 100 students. She became involved in a plan for an integrated, multi-age model that included all students and five teachers working together on new curriculums.

In her new role as copresident of the district's teachers union, Linda wanted to improve working relationships among teachers, administrators, and community members. Through discussion and experimentation, she sought to enlarge her focus to include using her leadership role to garner public support for education in her town. Finally, she aimed not just to improve working conditions for teachers, but to achieve the goals of the district strategic plan, which held important implications for quality education for students. What appeared in our conversation were professional projects for individual teachers' students that also promised to improve school experiences for all students.

## Change in School Culture

All of these project proposals displayed an overarching concern for meeting the diverse learning needs of students. As the team began to share reflections on one another's inquiry, however, they discovered something else they shared that was critically important: *The potential for expanded opportunities to improve student learning was dependent on the context of the school.* What if Ginny could engage all teachers, especially early education specialists, in an inquiry about the best practices related to how students learn to read? Could these teachers collaboratively explore new theories in order to investigate their own practice? Could Holly engage all faculty and students in a collaborative process of determining the musical focus for the year and build units of study integrating music into the larger curriculum? Could Elizabeth investigate alternative ways of conducting IST meetings and construct follow-up activities that would engage more faculty in helping to define student problems? Were there more collaborative ways of framing these problems and developing solutions? Could Barbara provide more support and direction to the enrichment program so that it could be expanded to include more students in the K–3 multi-age team? Could Linda, in her role as union copresident, find different ways to support teachers through their professional association that would engage more community support for schools and students?

The teachers soon realized that they all held a vision of a more collaborative and supportive work environment than they had originally thought. More important, they knew that none of their projects would get off the ground if more teachers were not included in the collaborative problem-solving process within the school.

## Teachers as Leaders

Concern with school culture led inevitably to an examination of the teachers' roles in that culture. As the team's dialogue evolved, all the teachers moved beyond the bounds of their own work into the broader issue of themselves as teacher-leaders. Although each teacher's individual project was conceptualized to improve learning for students, its actual evolution expanded to include exploration of school culture *and* her own capacity as a teacher-leader to affect that culture. In the end, the questions that defined the problem-based school development process for individual projects also served as the organizing framework for the team's inquiry into leadership. Viewing teachers' need for self-directed learning *and* their concerns for students as complementary tendencies formed the basis for this team's PBSD cycle. Framed in broader terms, their individual growth as adult learners complemented the school's development as an organization (see fig. 2.1).

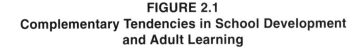

**FIGURE 2.1**
**Complementary Tendencies in School Development**
**and Adult Learning**

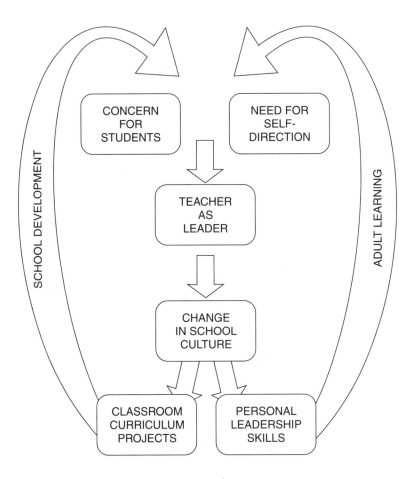

# Building Our Capacity for Learning

The first round of problem solving created new energy and enthusiasm and gave direction to the team. The teachers decided to explore the concept of "teachers as leaders" and to examine their roles as teacher-leaders in the school. What did it mean to be a teacher-leader, and how could they provide more leadership at the school level? How would teacher-leader skills empower them to contribute to the development of more collegial work relationships in the school? Could they remain participants in the process, building and constructing new models for student learning, rather than serving as persons "in charge" of change efforts?

Turning back to our easel and using the four focusing questions from problem-based school development, we began to plant the seeds that eventually grew into our "teacher leadership tree" (see fig. 2.2). The language of teacher leadership that developed moved away from the more traditional pathways for discussing leadership to embrace a new sense of connection among leadership issues. The branches of the tree connected personal characteristics, interrelational skills, institutional constructs, and leadership roles that defined these teachers' understanding of teacher leadership. From this brainstorm of ideas, they identified the leadership skills they believed were necessary to build community in their school and to improve learning for students. Their brainstorming also defined the work of their team for the coming year.

Over the next school year, the five teachers in the Teachers as Leaders strand participated in and completed a number of projects that embraced new forms of adult learning and professional development:

- *Monthly cohort team meetings* brought the five teachers together either before or after school to discuss shared readings they selected based on a different theme each month. The themes for these "book talks" came from the "teacher leadership tree" and encouraged discourse and reflection about what it means to be a teacher-leader.

- *Reflective dialogue sessions* held periodically at one another's homes allowed the teachers to share progress reports and problems related to new projects each had initiated. They solicited feedback and gathered support, developing a strong ethic of care for one another and for their independent work in the school.

- *A professional resource center* was developed and organized by the teachers in the school library. They used team resources to purchase professional books that they then cataloged and shared with colleagues in the school. Titles supported theories that inform collaborative work environments and collegial relationships among teachers.

## FIGURE 2.2.
## Teacher Leadership Tree

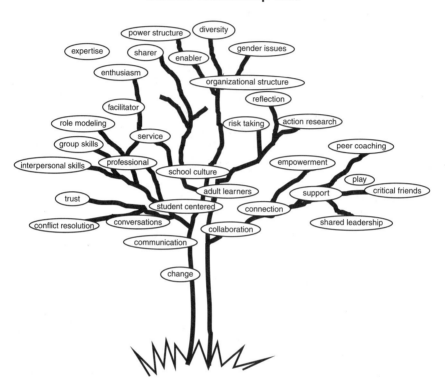

• *Professional resource binders* covered the broad themes the team explored over the year—teacher leadership, gender equity, action research, conflict management, peer collaboration, and organizational structure. Each binder contained relevant articles, research materials, notes and minutes from professional conferences, and other related artifacts. These binders were available to both the Teachers as Leaders team and to their colleagues.

• *Personal journals* constructed by the teachers included reflections on readings, attendance at conferences, cohort activities, and new instructional strategies they were implementing in their school. The journals documented the changes occurring in themselves and their schools.

# Refocusing on School Development

The Teachers as Leaders cohort team became the means through which team members interacted and coordinated their separate work. Their continuous dialogue and reflection served as the medium for much of their professional learning. As they shared stories and reflected in their journals, they were able to document the changes occurring not only in themselves, but in their schools as well. Several of these teacher-leaders found that the inquiry and collaborative skills they were practicing in their smaller cohort group carried over into their daily work as they collaborated to improve student learning throughout their school. Not only did they build a new context for adult learning, but they also improved their own conditions for teaching and learning, as their collaborative inquiries into new instructional practices fostered support from other colleagues inside the school.

For the Montpelier teacher-leadership team, changes within themselves and their school appeared to be almost simultaneous. As the school year drew to a close, new practices and structures that encouraged collaboration and collegial sharing and several curriculum changes that supported new learning opportunities for students began to take shape. Each teacher saw her PBSD project take form and become a reality in her school.

Elizabeth noticed that more members of the Instructional Support Team had taken responsibility for leadership at meetings. Also, teachers had arranged a number of peer-observation visits to one another's classrooms to share student-management strategies. "A highlight for me," stated Elizabeth, "was when we were able to observe each other and give specific feedback. We learned how to be challenged by observations, and not threatened."

After a summer of planning, Barbara's five-member multi-age team implemented a new program called "Structured Enrichment," which occupied a block of time each week of the school year. The program rotated multi-age clusters of students through a series of activities every five weeks. Teachers and students constructed and organized the activities around various themes, including Science Discovery, Computers, Paper-Making, Music, and Continents.

Ginny reported that a group of primary teachers from the school had organized an Early Literacy Intervention and Best Practices Team that met together on Friday mornings to investigate how to provide the most effective literacy instruction for children. Ginny also revealed plans for a schoolwide Book Sharing Center for beginning readers.

Holly's quest to work more collaboratively and interactively with students and faculty unfolded into a schoolwide interest in classical music. This interest expanded to the wider community, eventually including an ongoing partnership with a local conductor from the University of Vermont orchestra. Interest in classical music, composers, costumes, and ways to integrate all music into the curriculum came to inform classroom lessons. Classroom teachers and students also began to take on more leadership roles and responsibilities for developing and presenting school music performances.

As Linda began to work more collaboratively with faculty, board members, and the community in her role as union copresident, she organized a special meeting on education, titled "Montpelier at the Crossroads." The entire community was invited to attend this meeting to help "shape the future vision" for the education of students. "What emerged," stated Linda, "is the importance of working collaboratively with the superintendent, school board, administrators, and union executive board to achieve the goals that we have set for our schools."

At year's end, not only were each of these projects described in each teacher's professional portfolio, but themes from analysis and reflection on problem-based learning were woven into their narrative stories. It became clear that they were "building community" (Barth 1990), constructing an environment in which adults interact and learn together. More important, these teachers felt encouraged that a new culture was slowly emerging in their school, supporting continuous professional inquiry and collaboration. As Ginny wrote in her journal,

> The fence is down. We are all on the same road. Through opportunities for reflection and analysis, I better understand why our PBSD group has been so successful and why our Friday morning "conversations" have been so successful. . . . Recognizing personal experience as a critical component of expanding our knowledge is so important.

Barbara offered a similar reflection:

> I am excited about the progress of our enrichment program, as I am about the way our cohort group has evolved and worked together. This has been a year of tremendous support as a teacher working collaboratively with other teachers in very different capacities.

## Lessons from the Cycle

A number of lessons emerged from the yearlong experience of the Teachers as Leaders team. These lessons will continue to guide the team's work as teacher-leaders:

• A clear but flexible process can involve teachers in self-directed inquiry in a way that also improves student learning.

• Partnerships that support problem-based institutes can serve as a catalyst for learning and for leading school change.

• Problem-based inquiry can enable teachers to pursue problems that they are intellectually curious about and also allow them to improve relationships with their students.

• Through the context of a yearlong institute, teachers can create a culture of caring and respect, building a foundation of support for continuous inquiry and reflection leading to substantive change in classrooms.

## Teachers *Are* Leaders

The Teachers as Leaders team had begun work that first summer without a clear problem in view. They knew only that they shared a sense that "teachers are not really expected to lead" in any conventional sense, although they also saw that leadership lies at the heart of what they do every day. The team started out with five separate project ideas and a vague idea of teachers as leaders. As team members reflected on the meaning of "teachers as leaders," they changed their name to "teachers as facilitators." Later, as they began to work on their projects and conduct their monthly "book talks" about leadership, they decided to rename themselves again, this time as "teachers as collaborators." By June, they had come full circle, only to find that they could now accept what they had believed all along: "teachers *are* leaders." When called upon to make their final presentation to other teams, they opened with the following reflection:

> We came in June to do something, be part of something. We had all decided to take on something new, to change what we had been doing. But, we didn't want to do it alone. A full year has passed. In this year we have grown to feel more comfortable with the term *leader*, as we are better able to define the characteristics of good leaders. We came to the group looking for external evidence of leadership, but have discovered our own internal strengths within.
>
> —*Montpelier Teachers ARE Leaders Cohort Group, 1996*

# 3

# DEVELOPING A
# PROBLEM-SOLVING TEAM

Jane Briody Goodman

I have long enjoyed sharing a coffee break with my friend and colleague Karen, from the English department, to talk about teaching techniques and strategies for dealing with students we have in common. Until several years ago, however, the departmentalized structure at our school—Essex High School in Essex Junction, Vermont—offered little opportunity for colleagues from two different departments to work together, apart from such brief "kaffeeklatsch" moments.

One morning, our conversation turned to our 9th grade students. We began to chat about the issues confronting freshmen in transition from small "sending schools," where everyone knew their names, to the much larger, impersonal high school setting. Ninth grade students seemed to spend their first year at a loss, sometimes suffering academically or socially. Clearly, the first year was a pivotal year for high school students, yet we at the high school were devoting little effort to making the transition work.

What if, we thought, our school made a conscious effort to ease the transition from middle school to high school? What are the greatest challenges for incoming freshmen? How would our school look if we addressed the concerns of our 9th graders in a more systematic manner? What steps would we take? Would we have any administrative or faculty support for our ideas? Were we seeing the freshmen in an accurate light? Did they, indeed, have some major transition challenges? What would it take to gather teachers from all the departments to confront the shared problems resulting from our perception of neglect in the freshman year? With this set of questions to spur us on, we were off and running! A little coffee break had turned into one of those "Eureka!" experiences that inexorably become a call to action.

Five years after we began to ask questions about the freshman year, the original members of what we now call the Freshman Collaborative could look back in wonder at what had become of our modest program. All of the original members, with the exception of a teacher who moved away, remained actively involved in the growth and development of the program. From 10 faculty members we had grown to 25, with others involved for special topics and thematic planning. Although various constraints sometimes frustrated our efforts, on the whole, we had enthusiastic support, and the collaborative was well incorporated into the fabric of the school.

## Partnership with the University

Our group spent the first two years working together without external support, developing a set of common expectations for students and working on interdisciplinary curriculum units. At the end of our second year, an agreement between the school district and the University of Vermont School of Education made our school a Professional Development School, offering a Problem-Based School Development Institute that teachers could enroll in for university credit.

The benefits of the university-school partnership are multiple. The university-required individual and team reports provide accountability for our process, encouraging us to reflect upon our work and to set goals. We have incentives to research new information and data. Team reports are shared with university and high school colleagues, and, as a result, new teachers ask to join the program. We, in turn, look to colleagues in other PBSD groups for their expertise in such areas as developing outcome-based assessment or designing thematic units.

Our university partners encourage their undergraduate and postbaccalaureate students to intern in our program. Professional Development School interns do some of the in-house research that we would otherwise be unable to do because of time constraints. Interns attend our meetings, tutor students our group identities as at risk, do record searches, and chaperone special events. With funds from the partnership, we have sponsored school social events, purchased supplies for thematic units, and paid for substitute services for occasional inservice meetings during the school day.

Working as a problem-based school development team, we have slowly assembled a fairly comprehensive support program for freshmen. More important, however, we have learned to work together as a team. Our name, the Freshman Collaborative, reflects our determination to work together to solve problems in the freshman year, however and whenever they appear.

Not every member of the Freshman Collaborative has enrolled in the PBSD Institute for university credit each year. After five years, veteran team members, feeling that they had defined "the problem" and become adept at working with 9th graders in various creative ways, continued to participate on the team as part of their contracted professional obligation to the district. For them, the Freshman Collaborative teamwork serves as their professional duty during the school day, an expectation of all faculty members. Teachers new to the team, however, are encouraged to consider participating as credit-seeking problem-based team members.

Since its modest beginning, the Freshman Collaborative has welcomed as a member any teacher who shares the team's concern for freshman students. The completely interdisciplinary and eclectic nature of the group makes it a microcosm of the faculty at large. With roughly the same number of men and women, the team now represents seven academic departments, two universities, administration, and support services. Ages range from 18 to 60-something, and teaching experience from 0 to 30-plus years. New colleagues and university interns have enlivened and challenged the group by the nature of their interests, academic focus, and perspective on freshman problems. They also bring talents that can support an appropriate solution. We have discovered that a successful problem-solving team focuses the special talents of each team member toward a common purpose; it celebrates individual contributions whenever they occur.

## Team Support for Individual Energy

During the first months of the program, Karen and I asked for collegial support from each of the major departments. A group of 10 faculty members began to meet weekly, with Karen and me as cofacilitators, to develop a plan of action for a special freshman program. Our initial idea was to select a group of 50 students at random who shared many of the same teachers. We designed a few thematic units that would fit into our content-area curriculum. We organized activities and field trips for our students and developed specific strategies for those needing special academic, emotional, or social attention.

In that pilot year we examined the success of our program both quantitatively and qualitatively. Using student and parent surveys, we studied factors such as percentages of our students on the honor roll at various points in the year and involvement in extracurricular activities, and we identified students at risk. From our small group, we tried to get a portrait of the larger class. At the end of the year we made recommendations to the administration for more global changes. This pattern of goal setting, evaluation, and recommendation has persisted in our work, but we have steadily expanded our vision of the "problem" and greatly increased our capacity to work on problems as a team.

During its first five years, the Freshman Collaborative learned to use problems to organize a team response in which each member could play a distinctive role, earning professional respect by asserting individual talent. If focusing entirely on the problem diffuses and depletes team energy, focusing on individual contributions generates new energy that carries the team forward. Figure 3.1 shows questions a team can ask to sustain individual energy while the team works on solving common problems.

## FIGURE 3.1.
## Questions and Guidelines to Sustain Individual Energy During Team Problem Solving

**In Problem-Based
School Development**

**In Team Formation**

**FOCUS ON THE PROBLEM**

**FOCUS ON THE PROBLEM SOLVERS**

**What do we already know?**

**Who are we?**
Celebrate the participants,
who they are, and what they bring.
Give each a voice. Give each a role.

**What do we need to know?**

**What's our shared purpose?**
Create a clear structure that leaves room
for unpredictable discoveries. Schedule regular
meetings that feature each participant. Build a
predictable agenda, with lots of room for "other"
concerns. Bring focus back to common
problems, common goals.

**How will we find out?**

**What steps can we take now?**
Take small steps with attainable ends.
Try anything once. Evaluate each effort.

**What solutions look best?**

**What are the results?**
Communicate progress widely.

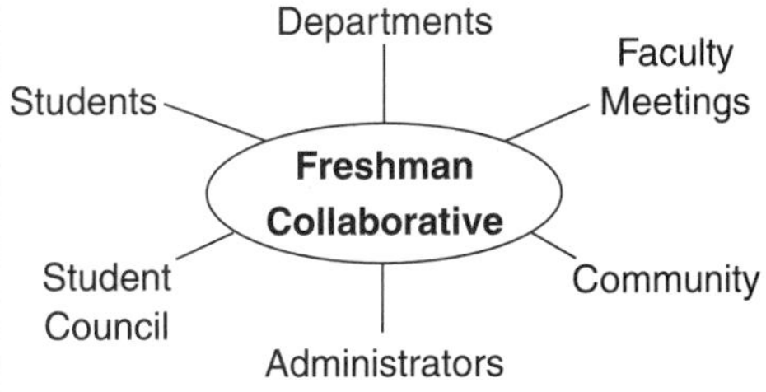

Departments

Faculty

Students

Meetings

**Freshman
Collaborative**

Student
Council

Community

Administrators

Propose solutions to wider community.

## Who Are We?

Individual energy drives team problem solving, and individuals bring to team meetings ideas that respond to their perception of a central problem. Consequently, the problems the Freshman Collaborative chooses to investigate and the solutions the team chooses to test depend on the particular perspectives and talents of individual team members. For example, several Freshman Collaborative members felt that community service projects would foster a sense of belonging to the freshman class. Projects evolved from opportunities individuals encountered in their lives outside of school. After a faculty member or a student approached the group with an idea for a community project, we worked together to brainstorm how to introduce the idea to our students and how to organize participation. Our work has ranged from food preparation at the Salvation Army to clothing drives and musical performances at senior centers. One spring students and faculty worked with the local recreation department to spruce up a local park for the summer. Individual faculty members joined specific projects that called on their particular talents and perspectives on the problem.

Our group has cultivated a strong sense of mutual professional respect, and we value healthy debate. Discussion of new ideas and proposals is generally thought-provoking and productive. We have learned to compromise to keep our focus.

## What's Our Shared Purpose?

Problem situations tend to change, particularly if a team of teachers works steadily to improve the situation. Rather than disappearing as solutions come forward, the problem tends to become more interesting as teachers learn to understand its complexity.

The Freshman Collaborative has slowly become a team working cooperatively behind the scenes on student transition issues for all 300-plus freshmen. Our group now serves as a collegial support group for 9th grade teachers as well as a "twin" organization for colleagues from other schools who visit to discuss issues ranging from block scheduling to strategies for students at risk. With confidence growing each year, we tackle new areas while building on our established programs.

The ability to respond to an expanding array of problems depends on developing a predictable and reliable structure for teamwork. During the school year, the collaborative meets for one hour each week. We also meet quarterly outside of school and hold two or three planning sessions during the summer. At the summer meetings we set goals, refine the structure for meetings, and choose roles within the group. We plan our 9th grade orientation program and the open house for parents of freshmen. High school upper-classmen called "peer helpers," working with university interns and tutors, play a key role in this informal evening of small-group question-and-answer sessions. We also define strategies for communicating with parents, colleagues, and the community-at-large during the coming year. Beginning in September, we include time in each week's agenda to begin planning community service projects and freshmen-only events.

## What Steps Can We Take Now?

Although it is tempting to take on a whole problem situation at once, a successful problem-solving team works incrementally toward a comprehensive solution that may not be imaginable when a team first forms. Progress depends on testing one idea at a time and fitting good ideas into an emerging pattern. For example, as members of the collaborative learn both about the problems of freshman transition and about solutions that fit or fail, the size of our focusing problem continually expands. At the end of our first year of work on integrated curriculum for a small group, student and parental response dictated that we change our program format. Parents expressed the wish that the program be more inclusive. Students preferred to be in classes with a broader group of their 9th grade peers. Our second and third years therefore included interdisciplinary studies for larger groups of freshmen.

Many new teachers have joined the program since its inception. We have reflected, critiqued, and assessed our work on an ongoing basis. In biannual meetings we review attendance patterns at events such as the parent open house, the freshman social events, and the tutorial and exam review sessions. We look at the academic and social data gleaned by reviewing academic records at every report card period and at the number of students deemed at risk whom we have referred to school support personnel. Based on our information and review of our "action steps," we make decisions about activities and approaches for the coming months.

## What Are the Results?

Success breeds success. Succeeding in one small step prepares the way for further steps. During its first five years, the Freshman Collaborative tried several experiments that are now fixed features of the high school program.

*Common expectations.* We worked together initially to develop common expectations for students in our classes. Coming to the high school from one of five different sending schools and often having six to eight different high school teachers, freshmen cited confusion about what was expected of them in make-up work, absences, homework due dates, and other classroom "administrivia." The disparity in classroom expectations provided an "out" for students who did not want to assume responsibility for doing work in a timely fashion. Teachers found themselves in a record-keeping nightmare, trying desperately to track down students for make-up work near the end of the marking period.

After many hours of discussion, we agreed upon a list of common, basic expectations to be implemented in our classes. We outlined clear guidelines for all of our freshman classes. Parents and students signed an agreement to uphold the guidelines. Teachers provided periodic reminders of these expectations to students. After successful piloting, these guidelines were adopted as school-wide expectations. Now we rarely need to discuss these issues with our students. Students acknowledge their responsibility to do their work on time or to accept the consequences. We accept no late homework and have clear, consistent expectations for work missed due to absences. Teachers are free to devote their energies to other matters.

*Instructional support.* We serve as an Instructional Support Team for students whom we have identified as at risk academically, emotionally, or socially. We have developed formalized action steps—strategies for communicating our concerns among teachers sharing the student, as well as with parents and school support personnel. These steps include initial brainstorming sessions among teachers to determine best practices with individual students. We also search records to see if the behavior is new or ongoing. A faculty "captain" is chosen for each student at risk. This person contacts parents and support personnel and often arranges conferences with the student.

For the last few years we have routinely identified from 17 percent to 22 percent of our freshman class as being at some risk during all or part of the 9th grade year. Naturally, this process was much easier when the Freshman Collaborative first began and we all shared only 44 students. An ongoing goal for the collaborative includes getting more assistance to more students in a more timely manner while overseeing the interests of the majority of the students in the freshman class.

*Organizational strategies.* Thanks to the initiative and encouragement of collaborative members from the guidance department, our group has worked with freshman students on time-management and organizational strategies, building leadership qualities and identifying learning styles. One year we helped to initiate the Get-A-Life portfolio program, which encouraged freshmen to begin thinking about both their four-year high school plans and their career options. With the aid of their guidance counselors, students were trained in learning styles and completed a personal analysis of their learning strengths and challenges. They then looked at strategies for working with their challenges and made preliminary four-year high school plans based on their goals and strengths. Teachers have access to these portfolios and have learned a lot about their students based on the students' self-analyses. Students continue to contribute to, review, and refine their portfolios during their high school years.

*Interdisciplinary studies.* During our first year we developed interdisciplinary units about several aspects of nearby Quebec province. Our students examined issues ranging from energy development to government, history, language, and culture. The units culminated in a trip to Montreal, where students actively engaged in such hands-on activities as estimating and measuring the water flow of the St. Lawrence River through the Lachine Canal and participating in a treasure hunt focusing on Canadian artists in the Museum of Fine Arts.

In our second and third years we designed interdisciplinary programs for the entire freshman class that examined the abstract concepts of hope and truth. With funds from local districtwide incentive grants as well as statewide corporate-sponsored funds, we were able to invite guest speakers, host artists-in-residence, and purchase materials to design artwork that is on permanent display in our school. A more recent effort was an interdisciplinary exploration of the theme of Energy: Physical, Creative, Spiritual. Teachers generate the topics for our thematic work based on their interests and curriculum dictates. Individuals seek grants with support from the team.

*Building collegiality.* From scheduling issues to special education regulations, we have learned firsthand the complexity of managing a large high school. Our conversations with administrators and support personnel have broken down barriers and fostered collegiality.

## Developing Administrative Support

Most high schools have no tradition of teacher-led change, and the Freshman Collaborative's early experience confirmed the presence of formidable barriers to such change. In our first year, we requested that the principal schedule a common planning period for the team, during which we would organize our activities. This request was denied, calling our commitment into question and leaving us wondering how far our energies could stretch. The problem of freshman transition was real in our experience. Teachers from all the subject areas recognized it as an important issue. But the tight high school schedule made no provision for a team of teachers to face and solve a problem they shared. We met, nevertheless, and, after one pilot year we were granted planning time and administrative support.

The time was right for change from within. Our faculty was fed up with top-down management and resistance from several colleagues. When given the opportunity to develop a program within the context of a graduate-level course and to earn academic credit, even funding, for problem solving, we were off and running. The Problem-Based School Development Institute was an incentive to further our work in a more formalized manner. In addition, our statewide recertification process changed to include credit for local initiatives, and it encouraged action research in professional development. A change in the school administration brought further encouragement for our initiatives. The administration has now clearly communicated to us that we have an important place in the school, that leadership is to be shared, and that faculty members who communicate and work for change on behalf of students are valued and rewarded. We, in turn, thrive on the support and en-

42

couragement provided us by school administrators who facilitate our work. Thus, many professional and emotional incentives encourage involvement as a team member and a school leader.

When we ask for common planning time, it is scheduled. When we pilot thematic programs or policy changes, our efforts are applauded and encouraged. The administration often consults us regarding schoolwide issues. Special educators and guidance personnel have sought a partnership with the teachers in the collaborative. This support has fostered a sense of confidence and leadership in all of us. We keep colleagues in our seven departments informed of our activities and bring ideas and concerns to the faculty senate and school council. Our members are encouraged to attend conferences, visit other schools, and receive training that we feel would help us to do a better job.

## Preparing for the Future

Now when Karen and I get together for coffee, we occasionally reflect on the factors that have contributed to the success of the Freshman Collaborative. Undeniably, we have made mistakes, had some flops. We have sat at a freshman dance with as many chaperones as freshmen and wondered if it was all worth it. We have encountered challenges to our goal of interdisciplinary work and have had to work through some scheduling glitches in order for all team members to be free during the same period. Karen went off to teach in Poland for two years, leaving the rest of us to flail about a bit, slowly acquiring some of her organizational skills. Ultimately, however, we have learned that our common commitment to our students and to one another keeps us meeting week after week, year after year.

We certainly cannot predict what the future holds, but for now, we can be fairly certain that one key factor has contributed to the success of this program: It has worked because it is ours. The program is an initiative based on a common concern broad enough to involve all sorts of people with all sorts of interests. We meet voluntarily and enjoy the support and nurturing of our school and university partners. We have created a "flexible structure," but one with enough order to provide continuity. The Freshman Collaborative team members experience leadership and partnership in the school community. We share a sense of belonging, fun, humor, and celebration.

As the winter skies close in and I contemplate a freshman project to clean up a park next spring, there is a tap on the door. It's Paul, a colleague from the practical arts department. "I know that I'm not a member of the Freshman Collaborative team," he begins, "but I have an idea that I'd like to explore with some of the teachers at your next meeting. You see, I've been interested in totem poles and the history that they tell through art. I'd like to make an Essex totem pole with some of the freshmen . . . " And so it goes.

# LEADERSHIP THROUGH DIALOGUE

KARIN K. HESS

> We must not cease from exploration. And the end of all our exploring will be to arrive where we began and to know the place for the first time.
>
> —*T.S. Eliot*

When I began teaching more than 20 years ago, staff development for teachers and school leaders was *much* simpler to define. Generally, the principal, as leader, decided the direction the school was headed and what professional development—or "training" as we called it then—was necessary to get us there. Then, all teachers participated in the inservice activity whether they needed or wanted it. Simple, right? There was little or no follow-up to these one-shot workshops, and rarely did the content or strategies presented ever find their way into full classroom implementation throughout the school.

Today, current literature suggests that professional development needs to provide depth of content knowledge, engage teachers intellectually, take a variety of nontraditional forms, be codesigned with teachers, and offer some ongoing support for implementation. This shift in the type of learning that teachers now need to engage in, in order to provide a "world class" education for their students, has also caused many administrators, like me, to wonder just what their new role in nurturing teacher professional development should be.

As the new director of curriculum at Addison Northeast Supervisory Union in Bristol, Vermont, responsible for planning the district's professional development activities and coordinating curriculum revision, I decided that being open to a professional development model that teachers felt was meaningful to their work would be my first step in supporting the teams involved in problem-based school development. This model would also open the door to my own new learning about how to "grow" leadership that supports change within a school system.

After two years of work with PBSD teams, I came to see my work as district curriculum coordinator as having two phases:

1. Supporting team leadership—forming relationships with team members and encouraging dialogue and reflection about team process, expectations, and progress.

2. Cultivating leadership density—recognizing leadership potential and weaving connections among teams so teachers can acknowledge their own leadership in shaping a shared vision of where the system is headed.

If forceful speaking was the key skill in the old model of school development, listening is the essential factor for success in PBSD. Teaching leaders to lead occurs best through dialogue and inquiry, an ongoing conversation about the diffusion of instructional leadership within a school system. So, during the school year, as teachers learned more about how to solve a complex, shared problem, I began to observe the PBSD process—and discovered that teams were developing a concept of leadership within their schools that emphasized their own responsibility for leading curriculum change, rather than the formal leadership of principals and administrators in distant offices.

# Listening to Support Team Leadership

Ellie and Susan, primary teachers at the Lincoln Community School, had already worked for a year as a PBSD team when I first met them. They had just begun their second year together in June. After reflecting on current needs, they decided to explore ways to expand their existing two-year unit of study of the Lake Champlain Basin into a third year involving the real-world classroom. Their inquiry plan outlined the need to develop a continuous study beginning in Ellie's 1st grade class and extending to Susan's 2/3 multi-age classroom—so students who started with Ellie would not repeat activities in Susan's class, but rather would build upon their previous experience during the following two years. Within this small team, a vision for learning was forming for virtually half of the school's six-year curriculum.

I arrived at the school early one morning in August—just in time to proofread a grant proposal that Ellie and Susan had written to support their emerging curriculum project. Developing the grant proposal was just one of the many activities they would document for the PBSD course. In our conversation that first day, I learned that Ellie and Susan had already spent much of their summer visiting museums, interviewing park naturalists and local historians, attending workshops, and locating related literature and resources to support their integrated unit of study.

For Ellie and Susan, forming a team enabled them to create a special relationship for constructing meaning about a new curricular model for continuous learning for their primary students. Throughout the yearlong PBSD course, they would share experiences as team members, building mutual trust and synergy and creating momentum for their continued work together. They would also interact and form relationships with the other teams working through the PBSD process. In short, they were developing a sense of community that would begin to formally and informally expand to other staff members at their school.

Surely, Ellie, Susan, and the other 10 teachers from the district who had registered for the Problem-Based School Development Institute did not do so with the intent of taking on a leadership role in school development; they became involved with their teams because they shared a vision for improved teaching and learning and felt that they could work together to solve a common problem.

Unwittingly, this also became their opportunity to change the school and school district culture and to further develop their own leadership skills.

As I listened to Ellie's and Susan's enthusiastic ideas and explanations, I realized that one of my new roles in support of all of the PBSD teams would be that of a "critical friend"—a term used by Michael Fullan and other school reformers to describe a nonjudgmental listener-clarifier (Fullan 1993). Rather than telling teams what they should be doing, a critical friend asks them to clarify their purposes and reflect upon their processes and goals. Providing support to all of the district's problem-based teams through the role of critical friend allowed me to discover and honor what was important to them, to assist them in accessing the necessary resources to complete their projects, and to help them to create some order for the energy they were generating by connecting individuals, teams, schools, and ideas. As critical friend, I became the weaver of the unifying thread.

What does critical listening look like? Just as there is no one formula for effective teaching, neither is there a formula for how to lead the conversation—through critical listening—so that it deepens understanding for all participants and moves people to sustain their activity and commitment. In general, however, I began to rely on my classroom skills for promoting inquiry and active listening. I began simply, with *variations on paraphrasing,* to be sure that I understood what people were telling me about their projects, followed by *clarifying questions.* For example, I might start with, "Let me see if I have this right: You are interested in using a range of children's literature for students to expand their knowledge of the history of transportation and navigation. How does this all fit with the rest of the curriculum? Does this also become part of the social studies and language arts units of studies, too? Will you assess skills and knowledge in all areas? Or just some?"

Next, I might pose questions in order to *discover the team's goals for the short term* ("What do you want students to do with this information? How will your students demonstrate understanding? Will they self-assess?") and the *long-range intent or impact* ("Does this lay the groundwork for later studies or skills this year? Or next year? What do you hope is the long-term impact of these experiences? Do you expect that they will want to involve family members in the project?").

Another path of questioning to explore might be to *encourage reflection* upon what has happened in the past—what the problem is that they are solving ("What made you want to change what you were doing in the past? What data did you look at? What was it that students were not doing well under the old system? What else have you tried?")—and *encourage a search for patterns* in the future ("How will you know if it works? What will it look like if this is successful? What do you think will make the difference?").

From these initial, clarifying dialogues, team members and I were then able to expand the conversations about ongoing projects and be much more articulate when speaking with principals, with other teachers and staff, and with district curriculum teams—connecting the team's work to the broader work of schools and the district. Telling stories about how projects are evolving, about how team goals fit with school goals, and about how team learning benefits other aspects of the system can plant the seeds of widening interest and inquiry.

The important first step, critical listening, builds a relationship of trust between us as professionals and gives me opportunities to validate the work—both the successes and challenges—that teams accomplish as they take on more responsibility for their learning and for school improvement. In addition, I have come to realize that time limitations potentially reduce my access to teams working in different schools, and I alone cannot sustain all of the team energy being generated in my district. Talking about shared leadership with teams has given rise to another new role for me—finding ways to connect teams and their work to the other teachers in their schools, finding ways to nurture their leadership activities through dialogue and reflection.

# Weaving Connections to
# Cultivate "Leadership Density"

How do we increase the number of problem-based teams so that more teachers become leaders who share a common direction? With the success of the first year's projects behind us, principals, first-year leaders, and I began to talk with teachers and support staff informally about using PBSD to carry out aspects of the school action plans and curriculum development. Many had been involved in some way with the first year's teams and were interested in continuing the work that had begun. And, as I began to look for leadership potential, it jumped out at me! Administrators can move an idea forward by simply recognizing leadership potential where it comes up and connecting the work of a team to similar work being carried out elsewhere in the district or school.

Dialogue among PBSD teams increases the perception that teams share a single direction, despite the fact that they are not being led by any single individual. "Leadership density," a phrase coined by former Vermont superintendent Ray Proulx, describes what can happen when leading a school through the change process becomes a collective endeavor. Density generally begins to develop when a few teachers take on nontraditional leadership responsibilities and by their example begin to create a culture that nurtures teachers as educational leaders. Similarly, the idea of "roving leadership" described by Max De Pree, former CEO of Herman Miller (in Wheatley 1992), suggests that for any model of change to become fully operational within an organization, many leaders must emerge throughout the learning community to share, support, and sustain the vision. The following examples illustrate how PBSD can spread.

*Alternative delivery models for special services.* Late in the spring of the first year of PBSD in our district, I attended a regional special education conference with a broad-based planning team (composed of parents, teachers, paraprofessionals, and administrators) from our high school. Our purpose was to explore some alternative delivery models for special education services and develop an action plan to increase the effective use of paraprofessionals and continuity of curriculum for students. Most members of the team had experienced frustration with many of the ideas that had been tried in the past.

By early afternoon, two things were clearly evident: (1) people were willing to work together and felt that a common vision was beginning to take shape; (2) there was no way that an action plan would be developed in the little time left that day. Teachers who had heard good things about the PBSD teams during the year suggested that this "problem" would be a perfect PBSD project for the coming year and asked if they could recruit others to begin work during the summer for the following school year. All I had to do was say yes, clarify how the work could be carried out, and the ball was rolling.

*Tasks for integrating science, mathematics, and technology.* Our high school recently merged several departments, eliminating the traditional role of department chair in favor of a coordinator for several departments. John, the former science department chair, became the new coordinator of the mathematics, science, and technology department. He came to me in the fall shortly after school started, asking for support for a full-day retreat for all of the teachers in his department so that they could explore ways to work together in their different curricular areas. They had had a retreat a couple of years ago, he told me, and it had been quite successful in bringing the department together as a team and getting them to make some decisions. I agreed to find the resources to support his request and left it to the teachers to plan with John how they would use their time.

What came out of that day, run by the teachers and facilitated by John, was a commitment by all to develop, within the existing high school courses, problem-solving portfolio tasks that integrated math, science, and technology in meaningful ways. When John reported back to me on the progress they had made, I slipped into my role as critical friend, asking him if I could meet with teachers during the next department meeting to clarify what actions they were going to take and to help them locate resource people who could guide their work. John's initiative became a PBSD team designing integrative tasks for students in mathematics, science, and technology courses.

*Standards-based curriculum.* Our high school parents had been asking us to make the curriculum more challenging and to better articulate how we assess learning. While John's department was exploring math/science/technology integration, many other teachers at the high school expressed an individual desire to work in small teams with a mentor to revise their own courses. With an inservice day approaching, principals began to discuss with the staff development committee how that day could be used. It was decided that Margaret, a veteran teacher with a great deal of expertise in differentiating curriculum for gifted students, would present a half-day workshop on developing critical thinking skills. Unlike the workshops of yesteryear, teachers would be asked at the end of the presentation if they wanted to continue working to upgrade their courses and develop standards and assessments. Margaret's workshop gave birth to a large PBSD team focusing on standards and higher-level thinking skills.

Recognizing the connections between PBSD teamwork and calls from the community for more rigorous curriculum, the high school principal invented a motto that we now use to focus school policy and aim new initiatives at increased academic rigor: "Challenge for All" became a motto for members of the whole school community to use in shaping their plans for the future. When the second year of PBSD began, not just the PBSD teams, but *all* the faculty had developed syllabuses for their courses that described content and learning expectations for all students. Most courses included tasks that required students to demonstrate what they had learned. Many teachers had developed grading rubrics that students could use to gauge the degree of their success in culminating projects. Plans began to take shape for developing a graduation portfolio for seniors. The school board asked the principal to develop next year's budget request to support "Challenge for All." Leadership that began in small PBSD teams was becoming schoolwide.

During our first year of problem-based school development, 12 teachers represented six teams from four schools. As we began year two, participation expanded from 12 teachers to more than 60 team members, representing all six schools in the district. Most of the original 12 teachers expanded their work to include other teachers or other initiatives during year two. Teams that include teachers, paraprofessionals, and administrators now link their "problems" to the school district's five-year strategic plan, addressing early literacy, standards-based curriculum and assessment, and delivery of services to special needs students. Although most participants are taking the PBSD course for credit, a significant number of others are becoming involved without seeking credit so that they can continue to work with colleagues on shared challenges.

## Growing Leadership

Since becoming an administrator, I have come to realize that the medium is the message: If we want teachers to aim teaching toward student performance, to individualize to meet diverse needs, and to practice learning through collaboration, we have to make sure professional development activities are consistent with those purposes. If we truly want teachers to lead school change, then perhaps PBSD can support and nurture teacher leadership as school change evolves.

My role as an administrator has been to become a design consultant, connecting one innovation to the next and emphasizing the emerging patterns in teaching and learning among different schools. I am becoming a teacher of leaders whose numbers grow with each success. To grow leadership in a whole district, I support the work of individual teams, but also urge them to connect their work to the larger vision emerging throughout the district schools.

The success and expanding interest in problem-based school development can be attributed in part to the impact that teacher-leaders have had on their colleagues and the support that they have been given to continue their work. While we may not solve all of the challenges we face, we are constructing a new model for leadership that we hope will someday include everyone. Managing an increasingly dense leadership environment means learning to manage increasing complexity.

5

# PLANNING INSTITUTES:
# THE MEDIUM IS THE MESSAGE

Nancy A. Cornell

H elping teams of educators investigate and solve a problem for their own schools and classrooms is surely the main task an administrator must undertake in managing a Problem-Based School Development Institute. Helping teams of teachers shape their solutions so they contribute to the development of a district organizing plan becomes a second important priority. At Rutland Northeast Supervisory Union in Brandon, Vermont, we had already experienced one highly successful year with problem-based teams before we took on the challenge of aiming team projects toward emerging district goals. It was through that success that we began to discover a design for the yearlong institute that would help teachers connect their own work to an evolving sense of where the whole school district was headed. We found that getting a large number of teams to start their year together creates collective direction with momentum of its own. Bringing them together as the year progresses brings the surprise of recognition, as teams see themes from their work reflected and extended by other teams.

Like PBSD Institutes in other school districts, our institute had ended its first year with a celebration of team "solutions." These solutions appeared to have no connecting thread: a 3rd grade book and history on local Civil War events, a K–2 study of the stream running through town, a greeting card and snack business established by grades 3 through 6, and a standards-based alternative education program for 9th graders. Only a detailed look at this collection would disclose the seeds of a districtwide organizing vision: connecting school to the community, emphasizing student performance, and increasing student direction over learning. If I, as district curriculum coordinator, were the only district educator to see coherence in team accomplishments, how likely would it be that we could continue developing in these new directions? Our Problem-Based School Development Institute, with 135 teachers enrolled, needed a way to let teams see the themes that held their work together.

The first-year teams had generated enormous energy in their schools, but few had recognized the connections between their projects or the implications of their work for district goals. Long before we began to work with PBSD, we had established learning goals through community forums across our district, but we had emphasized the importance of local direction and full participation by teachers. Our curriculum development process had abolished district curriculum committees and instead called on full faculties of every school to make curriculum decisions together. We had developed a districtwide strategic planning framework based on our learning goals, but had called on each school community to fill in that framework with its own strategies for helping all students succeed.

We had designed the central office strategic plan to support each of the school plans. The supervision and evaluation system turned much responsibility for professional growth over to teachers. We had created an assessment design and an implementation plan for that design, based on our learning goals, but we had left most of the details of the plan up to each school faculty. Still, until we stumbled on problem-based school development, our professional development offerings were largely of the "open head, insert knowledge" variety: 3-credit graduate courses with a preordained syllabus and an instructor who received district funds in return for imparting information to our teachers, who enrolled hoping to gain knowledge that might improve their ability to improve student learning.

# Redesigning the PBSD Institute

For the second round of PBSD, we decided to start anew and focus on some common goals. To design the second institute, we gathered a group of 12 teachers, many of whom had been members of problem-solving teams the previous year. We began with the question, "What should teaching and learning look like when we're 'there'?" and the subsequent questions, "What obstacles get in the way of our being 'there' now?" and "What would help us get 'there' sooner?" The teacher planning team soon reached consensus on these questions, and we began our work with this consensus as our guide.

The planning team members who had participated in the previous year's institute spoke with enthusiasm about the synergy that had resulted from that experience. The group agreed that a problem-solving format should be the foundation of the design, but as we began to get down to details, the coherence/chaos struggle reared up to challenge us all. Surprisingly, many of the teachers in the room felt it was important to lay out more stringent requirements for teams.

"Everyone should be required to use information technology with students as part of the outcome of this institute!" said one.

"What if the problem a team takes on is more about faculty communication or school governance than it is about designing a learning experience for kids?" I asked. "For them, this requirement wouldn't fit, would it?"

"Everyone should be required to attend a session on team-building. And another on using community resources," said another.

"What if the team members are already working well as a team?" I asked. "What if community resources aren't a solution that would help them solve the problem they've defined?" I asked.

"Each team *must* design a project around our new state standards! At least we can all agree on that," someone else insisted.

"Supposing the team is working in a school community that has not endorsed the state standards?" I asked.

These were intense, sometimes heated conversations. We all felt the need for some focus that would help guarantee that team projects would move our schools in a common direction. We each held strong beliefs about which school reform efforts held the most promise for moving our schools forward, but not everyone shared the same beliefs. And we all saw that imposing a particular focus on the new institute would run counter to the problem-solving framework that had succeeded in bringing us to this point. We needed to preserve team autonomy but also help teams recognize the contribution of their work to the general direction that had already emerged.

In the end, we discovered a modest solution. We would adapt the first three questions of PBSD to shape the beginning of the next year:

1. *What is the problem situation?* In announcing the second phase of problem-based school development, we would emphasize progress earlier teams had made toward a standards-based curriculum emphasizing student performance, technology, and community involvement.

2. *What do we need to know?* We would ask teams to describe a problem connected to established progress so their results would tend to be continuous with prior work.

3. *Where can we find out?* In our first gathering, we would surround the teams with local "resource people" whose expertise promised to extend what earlier teams had learned and to connect team inquiry to district policy directions enhanced by whatever state initiatives supported those directions.

## Enriching the Available Resource Pool

The first year of problem solving had created energy and an emerging sense of direction. The second would use these accomplishments as a starting place for new initiatives in a confirmed direction. We would create a resource-rich environment to start the second PBSD cycle, allowing teams to hook up with resource people representing district priorities and giving them access to the limitless pool of information outside our state.

The PBSD Institute would kick off with three days of team planning during the summer. We would infuse the gathering with resource people—12 to 15 consultants, some funded by a grant and others provided by the state or university—in the areas of team building, using community resources, standards-based curriculum design, curriculum design in selected content areas, problem-based learning, and information technology. We would ask the consultants to prepare presentations—but no participant would be required to attend any event. Beyond the presentations they offered, these same consultants would be available for individual team consultations ("office hours") during the three-day kickoff and would also be available via e-mail and phone during the year.

Team members would meet early on the first day to decide which presentations to attend. They would assemble a view of what they already knew. Then they would begin generating questions defining what they believed they needed to find out. They would send out "scouts" to find out which presentations, workshops, and consultants (if any) could help them with the inquiry part of solving the problem they had defined. The consultants would also join us for our follow-up meetings in the fall and spring. By surrounding teams with a rich assortment of consultants, we could place the teams in the wider environment of information without limiting their freedom to inquire. The curriculum coordinators and university representatives would spend the three days wandering among the teams, weaving connections between teams and with consultants where appropriate.

The idea of creating an "enriched environment" in which all attendance was optional seemed like a huge risk. What if no teams used the consultants we provided? What if our well-paid resource people sat around for three days drinking coffee with their feet up? "So be it," we said. For this to work, the teams—not the consultants, not the planning team, not the central office—needed to be in control of the problem-solving process. "Besides," someone on the planning team pointed out, "this is the same risk I took when I moved from a teacher-centered instructional style to one that was more student-centered. The medium is the message."

## Three Days of Constructive Chaos

As the school cafeteria filled with teachers and paraprofessionals, the size of the group and the challenge to our institute design was clearly apparent. How would this thing come together in a way that moved our schools in the directions that had been defined as key to improving student learning? As the teachers began their work, they sat with their teams. Resource people lined the walls. A network-wired computer lab waited down the hall. The design was complete. How visibly would it influence problem description and analysis?

Those three days seem a blur to me now. What I most remember, though, is running around like a madwoman from team to team, answering urgent questions, clearing up misconceptions about district initiatives and state standards, helping people connect with folks from other teams, bringing materials I had gathered for them during the spring, listening carefully to thoughtful problem statements and to new ideas on solutions and promising avenues of inquiry, sharing e-mail addresses, and offering "soft money" when promising ideas emerged that would require more resources than the institute reinvestment funds could cover. The three days were simply a highly compressed version of what I do all year.

During those three days, team members met together, sent individuals to particular workshops and to the computer lab to do Internet searches, and picked the brains of resource people during private "office hour" appointments. Amidst all that tumult, sure, some people got scared, some became frustrated. But mostly people felt a distinct thrill at finding themselves in the midst of such a flurry of professional inquiry and collegial opportunity. Curriculum coordinators, university representatives, and resource people could thread the teams together and point beyond the summer to helpful information to be gathered and digested as the year continued. When the last person left the building on the last day, I was physically and mentally exhausted—but I felt it had been the best professional development I had helped organize in six years as curriculum/staff development coordinator.

## Forming Order from Energy

Exhilarated as I was at the end of those three days, I still had doubts that team efforts would develop into projects that would move our schools in the directions we had established. But in subsequent meetings with teams once the school year began, my doubts disappeared. Standards-based unit design, community connections, and technology had permeated teamwork, as the following examples illustrate:

• A team working on study skills for 7th and 8th graders had designed a learning guide and assignment notebook that led to a wonderfully smooth start to the school year—and a gaggle of impressed and satisfied parents. The team's work and the work of a study skills team from another school in the district had been featured at a school inservice session at the start of the year and were completely in line with local and state personal development standards that focused on workplace skills.

• A high school team had undertaken the revision of several units of study for its interdisciplinary American Studies course, and for a Career English course. The team members' goal was to make both the content and the assessments standards-based. Their units and assessments zeroed in on particular communication and content standards in the *Vermont Framework of Standards for Learning*, a guide for teachers.

• Several elementary literacy teams had embarked on book-leveling (choosing books at various skills levels), assessment, and professional and paraprofessional development projects that aligned well with our district assessment plans and reading standards. Book-leveling would bring teachers and paraprofessionals together to further hone their skills in ongoing assessment to inform instruction and building students' repertoires of reading strategies.

• Members of an elementary math team had begun collecting and cataloguing problem-solving resources to help their classes improve skills in this area under the criteria of our state math problem-solving assessment. As part of their inquiry, team members planned to attend a workshop that would help them organize a family math night, and they arranged site visits to other classrooms in the state, with the purpose of gleaning ideas for great math programs from other teachers.

• Two guidance counselors had designed and implemented a peer counseling program for students that aimed to help students meet district standards in the areas of personal development and social responsibility. The counselors started their inquiry during the school year by attending workshops on the subject with a team of students, so they could create the program together.

No single conventional graduate course I could have organized would have accommodated such a variety of teachers' needs and interests. No workshop or conference I have ever attended or developed was so effective in connecting district directions and state resources to teachers' immediate concerns in ways that led to direct positive effects on children. Principals in schools where institute teams continue their work stop me in the hall to comment on the enthusiasm and energy they're witnessing as the teams pursue solutions to the problems they have defined. And this energy seems to have extended beyond the institute participants to other staff members.

## Elements That Promote Success

No model for school change, however successful in one place, is necessarily transportable to another. The success of any model depends on a stunning array of contextual factors that make cookie-cutter replication an iffy prospect at best. Still, our model for putting together a Problem-Based School Development Institute contains elements that are worthy of consideration for other places:

• *Involving teachers as planners.* Involving teachers as primary planners of the experience helped ensure that the model we developed would be responsive to the immediate professional needs of the participants.

• *Defining problems early in the process.* Asking teams to begin to define their problems while we were still in the planning stages enabled us to identify appropriate resource people to have on-site, ensured that teams would be ready to hit the ground running when the institute opened, and gave team facilitators like me a chance to collect documents and materials that might prove useful as the teams began the problem-solving process.

• *Including resource people in planning.* Involving the resource people in the last of our three planning meetings guaranteed that they understood our unorthodox design, including the notion that the teams, not the consultants, would be driving the train. Their involvement in the planning also gave us a chance to give them enough information on our local context (learning goals, alignment of these goals with state standards, histories of teams' previous work, etc.) so that they could prepare presentations and office-hour appointments in ways that helped teams connect their work to systemic, policy, and team work that was already under way.

Of course, our choice of resource people was also important. They were a conglomerate of teachers, university people, and consultants from the State Department of Education and the State Systemic Initiative funded by the National Science Foundation. Their areas of expertise reflected both team needs and systemic policy directions. All were folks whose work was well grounded in the day-to-day life of real schools. All had a deep understanding of their critical role as capacity builders, not simply as fonts of knowledge. Most important, they were willing to work as "optional" resources in an open format that would make preparation difficult.

Consistent follow-up and support of teams has also been a key element of this model. After the initial kick-off days, our teams work throughout the year, and inevitably they get stuck, get scared, get stalled. The school year begins, everyone gets incredibly busy, the team inquiry process turns up new questions and daunting obstacles. Each team has a facilitator (in our institute, this is the district curriculum coordinator) whose job it is to check in regularly and help teams troubleshoot. Facilitators also help teams keep school administrators informed about team initiatives and needs. In addition, all teams have access during the year to the resource people by phone, e-mail, and at follow-up gatherings. This follow-up helps everyone keep the faith, even when variables intervene (bomb scares, budget crises, contract snags, things that go bump in the night.)

In the end, the leap of faith in the PBSD model amounts to the risk of trust: a trust in professionals to identify key problems and carry out professional inquiry that will lead to solutions; trust that local and state policies developed through grass-roots inclusive processes will be useful to those who face kids every day; and trust that building the capacity of those closest to the children to define, research, and solve the problems they face. Yes, trust is the most important and most promising role that school administrators and state education officials can take on. Through this experience, I've begun to discover that the best professional development program must model the kind of teaching that lights kids on fire about learning. In the best professional development, the medium is the message.

# POLICIES SUPPORTING
# ADAPTIVE GROWTH

STEPHEN D. SANBORN AND JOHN H. CLARKE

> Change is a river,
> Sometimes rushing through treacherous rapids,
> Other times swirling in slow, deep eddies.
> Policies are the banks that guide a river,
> Not dams that impede the natural flow of water.
> —*Steve Sanborn*

Frequently, projects that problem-based school development teams develop to improve student learning interfere with existing patterns of practice or collide with existing aspects of schoolwide organization. While PBSD teams are building new ways for their students to learn, such things as bell schedules, grading practices, report cards, graduation requirements, discipline systems, and written curriculum stand firm to preserve established practice. The process of PBSD increases the natural tension between energy and order—the need for growth struggling with the need for stability, newer ideas straining to find a place within structures that support continuity. How can we develop policies that allow innovation to flourish in organizations that require some stability to survive?

In buildings bursting with energetic kids, adults fear chaos above all other threats. Often, we try to suppress the problems that arise in school life, rather than solve them. Consequently, the public school stands as a monument to predictable order, but not necessarily to the purpose for which it was established—appropriate learning for all students. The sun rises, buses roll, bells ring, students move quickly into assigned places, textbooks are opened—then more bells ring, buses roll again, the sun sets. We have created a structure in which neither students nor teachers have the time or energy to adapt to the problems that come up in a typical day. In short, we call for improvement but prevent change, a paradox that guarantees widespread frustration.

PBSD increases the level of energy available to support school change, further threatening the orderly structures that hold schools together. Previous chapters have included stories that illustrate the effects that PBSD can have on adult teacher development, professional colleagueship, school leadership, and school development. Each of the authors has struggled to create a successful balance between energy and order in a growing system, allowing professionals to work together for meaningful school change without destabilizing the whole system. Still, we should not try to disguise the potential for conflict, as team-led innovations crash into practices a school has developed to keep itself running. Schools experimenting with problem-based school development must develop policies and procedures that accommodate the destabilizing arrival of newer ideas.

## Collisions of Order and Energy

As the following examples illustrate, nothing can be more destructive to the prospects for school improvement than an administrative decision or school-board vote that overturns a year of energetic effort by a school development team.

*Curriculum policy and resource allocation.* A PBSD team at a local high school (not the Essex team described in Chapter 3) had spent a year developing a plan for a new 9th grade transitional program. Students from the incoming 8th grades would have the option of enrolling in a full-year, cross-disciplinary program taught by a team of four subject area teachers. By scheduling these teachers and students into a four-period block, the new program would open up time for extended inquiry by students—for using computer and library resources—and for extensive team teaching by participating teachers. The Freshman Year PBSD team had worked out the curriculum, created a basic schedule, and prepared a proposal for presentation to the school board. The proposal included a common planning period for teachers, replacing one duty period.

As the plan went forward, it aroused resistance at each successive level of school organization. If only half the freshman class experienced an interdisciplinary curriculum, sophomore teachers would not be able to assume prerequisite skills and knowledge among all their students. If teachers of freshmen were granted a common planning period, other personnel might end up with extra duties. A morning block of four periods would remove four teachers from the schedule of existing courses. The school board would have to fund replacement teachers for duties and stretch the limits of the existing teacher contract.

After months of excruciating discussion, the board and administration turned down the proposal; the 9th grade team disintegrated in frustration; members of the team, all of whom had exceptional reputations as teachers committed to change, withdrew into their separate classrooms and no longer expressed interest in school development. Unlike teachers in the Freshman Collaborative at Essex High School described in Chapter 3, these teachers began to avoid freshman classes because the board decision prevented them from solving the problems they needed to solve to work effectively.

*Personnel policy and professional development.* During a regular weekly meeting of a Professional Development School Governance Council, representatives of both the high school and the university were discussing strategies to make the PBSD Institute more user-friendly for teachers. In the past, teachers had been offered three graduate credits, earning traditional grades for their work. One teacher suggested that a pass/fail grading system might be more attractive. Everyone on the council agreed. The university representative said that this transition would be no problem for the uni-

65

versity, and everyone left the meeting feeling that this simple policy change would have a positive impact on the participation of teachers in the School Development Institute.

When this change was presented to the administrations in both the school district and the university, a number of policy restrictions emerged that discouraged the governance team from moving forward. First, according to school district policy, teachers were required to have a B grade or better to be reimbursed for a graduate-level course. A pass/fail grade would prevent teachers from receiving reimbursement. Next, the Local Standards Board (which governs teacher recertification in the state) questioned whether a pass/fail grade could result in credit toward recertification. Finally, the university agreed to offer pass/fail grades but refused to apply a pass/fail grade toward a graduate degree. Although this example may seem insignificant, it shows that a modest change in PBSD grading policy would have undercut the incentive that supported conventional professional development programs.

As these and other examples illustrate, the enormous weight of longstanding policy can overwhelm a team-generated initiative, bruising egos and straining professional relationships in the process.

## Policies Supporting Systems Adaptation

How can we create a system that will accommodate and even encourage an organic, self-generating process of school and professional development? We must first accept the assumption that the primary responsibility of policymakers is to create an environment that supports professionals who are willing to ensure higher learning for all students. Policy development should shift priority from the process of maintaining schools to the process of promoting student learning. Policymakers should focus their efforts on (1) gathering consensus on what students should know and be able to do, (2) reviewing existing policies to determine whether they support professional development activities that improve student learning, (3) making policy adjustments that support incremental change, and (4) monitoring and evaluating the impact of policy on student learning. Policy can be modified to allow continuous experimentation with the complex factors that interact to restrict learning.

Early forays into the process of PBSD have convinced us that established policy structures tend to restrict capacity to create meaningful change. Recognizing the struggle between energy and order in school development, many analysts have begun to reconceptualize the role of policymaking, so the processes that support change begin to receive as much attention as the processes that reinforce order. Change requires steady effort. Policy must accommodate the idea of making school development "steady work" in the daily routine of school life, rather than a sporadic effort on inservice days. Milbrey McLaughlin (1987) suggests that "we cannot mandate what matters to effective practice; the challenge lies in understanding how policy can enable and facilitate." Policy development should encourage and support long-term developmental growth in teaching and learning, resisting the temptation to freeze practices in place that maintain existing systems, suppressing the adaptations that flow from the ongoing work of professional teams.

Differences between problem-based school development and conventional graduate programming can strain policies established to support teacher development. Figure 6.1 compares conventional and problem-based development. As the figure suggests, conventional graduate-level programs for teachers presume that solutions to the most pressing problems in schools already exist in forms that can be taught and applied generally. PBSD, in contrast, assumes that teachers need to restructure existing knowledge in order to apply it successfully to specific problems unique to their schools. Teachers in conventional courses struggle to integrate knowledge created in another context into the complexities of their own classrooms. PBSD helps teachers use knowledge to construct a fitting response to specific issues in their own professional experience. We cannot use conventional teaching techniques to solve problems that emerge in different contexts. We need policies that support continuous, organic growth within teachers.

With these observations in mind, we offer the following guidelines for policy development:

• *Policy development should recognize the need for self-direction and peer support in adult learning.* Research and theory on adult development has produced four principles that policy should accommodate: as people mature (1) they become much less dependent and more self-directed; (2) they use their life experiences as learning

67

resources and to help establish identity; (3) their readiness to learn is closely related to the development tasks of their social roles; and (4) their learning is organized around problems rather than content (Whiting 1988). A fifth assumption suggested by Lieberman and Miller (1990) is that teachers need to collaborate in order to learn. The problems they face are not comprehensible from a single perspective. Teachers find that school development is much more rewarding and enjoyable and the results are of higher quality when they work in teams. We have found that conventional professional development programs have honored neither the needs of the adult learner nor those of the experienced educator.

• *Policy development should recognize that solutions to problems of teaching and learning are more likely to emerge in the classroom than the board room.* The solutions that teams of professionals devise usually accommodate the specific needs they recognize in their students, as well as the complex pressures of life in schools. Solutions developed by distant policymakers, on the other hand, tend to treat all problems the same way. They tend to oversimplify the dynamics that create classroom problems. They also tend to deprive teachers of access to their own adaptive capability, provoking resistance to change rather than involvement.

• *Policy development should recognize the critical role administrators play in supporting and guiding team-based change.* It should also address the changing roles of central office administration when the impetus for change comes from the bottom rather than the top of the educational power structure. Effective staff development seems to happen organically when teachers are given the opportunity to struggle with real problems found in the everyday challenges of public schools—and when administrators have the time and resources to support the solutions teachers want to develop. When administrative roles are cluttered with mechanics, required procedures, and endless organizational meetings, the quiet struggle of a faculty team is likely to go unnoticed. Without administrative recognition and support, emergent solutions to problems in teaching and learning die of neglect.

• *Policy development should support the emergence of leadership among professional teachers.* School development policy should encourage administrators to shift focus from formulating rules and directives to determining what is best for students, helping identify problems, and organizing teams to solve those problems. Schools

68

should become centers of critical inquiry where faculty and students have the opportunity to become learners and questioners. Emerging policy should encourage, support, model, catalyze, and collaborate rather than regulate, dictate, or direct.

### FIGURE 6.1.
### A Comparison of Conventional and
### Problem-Based Professional Development

| Conventional Development | Problem-Based Development |
|---|---|
| **PURPOSE** | |
| Purpose is imported from outside sources. | Purpose is discovered incrementally as the problem situation gains clarity and depth. |
| **LEARNING PROCESS** | |
| The learning process should be orderly and systematic. | Learning is necessarily sloppy, meandering, and recursive. |
| **CONTENT ACQUISITION** | |
| Learners try to acquire an organized body of information. | Learners adjust what they know to accommodate new information in a real world context. |
| **SOURCE OF LEARNING** | |
| Knowledge exists as an entity to be replicated in the learner. | Knowledge evolves as the perception of the problem situation changes. |
| **ORGANIZATION** | |
| Knowledge is organized to represent an existing model. | The individual must develop a personal explanation for a specific clinical situation. |
| **TEACHERS** | |
| Teachers present information and test to see whether it has been acquired. | Teachers support the discovery of relevant information, perspectives, and emerging solutions. |
| **ASSESSMENT** | |
| Tests and papers compare learning to predefined standards. | Final presentation fits new knowledge to a unique representation of the problem. |
| **DOCUMENTATION** | |
| Results are documented in terms of grades and degrees. | Findings and results are published in a professional portfolio and Internet file. |

69

• *Policies development should recognize the necessity of change rather than the requirements of stability.* Because schools support young people moving toward the gateway of adult responsibility, they must be flexible enough to respond to the changing needs that every generation of young people brings to school. Yes, the needs of society are predictable. We need a steady supply of new citizens who can direct their own lives, participate actively in democratic processes, and prepare the way for generations yet to come. Coming from vastly different backgrounds, however, young people themselves demand adaptive rather than formalized responses to their needs. We cannot predict the needs of coming generations in advance; instead, we must prepare teachers to respond energetically to the new problems that each new generation of students brings to school.

## Accommodating Chaos While Order Evolves

With many PBSD teams traveling on many different tracks, no individual can know exactly what is happening at any moment. As teams begin independent inquiry, educators with formal authority must give up control of the staff development process and accept the fact that they are no longer the authors of either knowledge or power, that learning in a changing situation is not necessarily orderly and systematic, and that their purpose is not to deliver an "organized body of knowledge" to teaching professionals, who actually need to learn how to construct knowledge for themselves. Policy cannot define "what is best" for professionals but must accept a more organic approach to change that is often sloppy, meandering, and recursive in its pursuit of emergent solutions.

Working with problem-based school development teams over several years in several districts, we began to see chaos theory, or complexity theory, as a source of both inspiration and insight. Everywhere they are found, complex systems—such as schools—are struggling to obey two conflicting tendencies, one that leads toward sustainable order and the other that produces new energy. Figure 6.2 depicts this struggle as it occurs in school development. The need for transforming energy is most apparent in the cries for reform we hear from the world outside—and in the outrage of students who don't fit nicely into existing structures. How can a school maintain and transform itself simultaneously to support learning for all the students?

### FIGURE 6.2.
### School Improvement Teams
### Professional Development Through Problem Solving

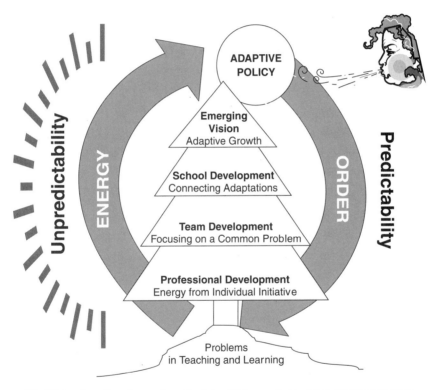

"Equilibrium is neither the goal nor the fate of living systems, simply because as open systems they are partners with their environment. . . . [O]pen systems have the possibility of continuously importing free energy from the environment and of exporting entropy. They don't sit quietly by as their energy dissipates. They don't seek equilibrium. Quite the opposite. To stay viable, open systems maintain a state of non-equilibr ium, keeping the system off-balance so that it can change and gro w" (Wheatley 1992).

Wheatley, M. (1992, 1994) *Leadership and the New Science: Learning About Organizations from an Orderly Universe.* San Francisco: Berrett-Koehler Publishers, Inc.

In complexity theory, the tendency toward order and the tendency to create energy are both self-limiting; too much energy leads toward chaos, a level of disorganization that cannot reproduce itself; too much order leads toward stagnation, congealed patterns of organization too inflexible to adapt to ongoing evolution in neighboring systems. In complexity theory, energy and order are not antithetical. They are two parts of one process—called growth, adaptation, or self-organizing renewal. Change depends on the regular appearance of fluctuations that challenge "business as usual," forcing established patterns to change.

As Margaret Wheatley describes the interplay of energy and structure, "The two forces that we have always placed in opposition to one another—freedom and order—turn out to be partners in generating viable, well-ordered, autonomous systems" (1992, p. 95). In Wheatley's view, problems represent a necessary disruption in the system, a signal that survival depends on adaptation. Problems reflect benign disequilibrium in the system—stressing the need to grow in new directions. Born in the dance of energy and order, growth, communication, and creativity are self-organizing responses to uncertainty, as is learning itself. If we allow problems to shape our conversations with one another, we will find ways to grow dynamically as one profession—inviting young people to join us as we struggle to understand and manage our own growth.

# REFERENCES AND FURTHER READINGS ON PROBLEM-BASED SCHOOL DEVELOPMENT

Aspy, D.N., C.B. Aspy, and P.M. Quinby. (1993). "What Doctors Can Teach Teachers About Problem-Based Learning." *Educational Leadership* 50, 7: 22–24.

Barrows, H.S. (1988). *The Tutorial Process.* Springfield, Ill.: Southern Illinois School of Medicine.

Barrows, H.S., and A.C. Myers. (1993). *Problem-Based Learning in Secondary Schools.* Monograph #1. Springfield, Ill.: Problem-Based Learning Institute, Ventures in Education, Inc., Southern Illinois School of Medicine and Springfield School District #186.

Barth, R. (1990). *Improving Schools from Within.* San Francisco: Jossey-Bass.

Boud, D., and G. Feletti. (1991). *The Challenge of Problem-Based Learning.* New York: St. Martin's Press.

Bransford, J.D., R.D. Sherwood, and T. Sturdevant. (1987). "Teaching Thinking and Problem Solving." In *Teaching Thinking Skills: Theory and Practice,* edited by J.B. Baron and R. Sternberg. New York: W.H. Freeman.

Bridges, E.M., and P. Hallinger. (1995). *Implementing Problem-Based Learning in Leadership Development.* Eugene, Oreg.: ERIC Clearinghouse on Educational Management.

Brown, J.S., A. Collins, and P. Duguid. (1989). "Situated Cognition and the Culture of Learning." *Educational Researcher* 18, 1: 32–41.

Central Vermont School Development Institute Consortium. (1995). *Central Vermont School Development Brochure.* Montpelier, Vt.: University of Vermont, School Development Institute.

Clarke, J.H. (1990). *Patterns of Thinking: Integrating Learning Skills in Content Teaching.* Boston: Allyn and Bacon.

Clarke, J., and R. Agne. (1997). *Interdisciplinary High School Teaching: Strategies for Integrated Learning.* Boston: Allyn and Bacon.

Clarke J.H., and A. Biddle (1993). "Designing Solutions to Problems." In *Teaching Critical Thinking: Reports from Across the Curriculum,* edited by J.H. Clarke and A. Biddle. Englewood Cliffs, N.J.: Prentice Hall.

Clarke, J., A. Friedricks, B. Nelligan, S. Sanborn, and A. Vilaseca. (May 1995). "Reform from Within: Gathering Available Support for a School/College Partnership." *NEASSC Bulletin* 5–9. (New England Association of Schools and Colleges, Burlington, Mass.)

Clarke, J., and S. Sanborn. (1996). "Team Guide for Problem-Based School Development." Essex Junction, Vt.: Chittenden Central Supervisory District. (Available from authors.) [A booklet guiding teams through the process.]

Cochran-Smith, M., and S.L. Lytle. (1993). *Inside/Outside: Teacher Research and Knowledge.* New York: Teachers College Press.

Cochran-Smith, M., and S.L. Lytle. (1996). "Communities for Teacher Research: Fringe or Forefront?" In *Teacher Learning: New Policies, New Practices,* edited by M.W. McLaughlin and I. Oberman. New York: Teachers College Press.

Cognition and Technology Group of Vanderbilt University. (1990). "Anchored Instruction and Its Relationship to Situated Cognition." *Educational Researcher* 19, 6: 2–6.

Dalellew, T., and Y. Martinez. (1988). "Andogogy and Development: A Search for the Meaning of Staff Development." *Journal of Staff Development* 9, 3: 28–34.

Darling-Hammond, L. (1994). *Professional Development Schools: Schools for Developing a Profession.* New York: Teachers College Press.

Drinan, J. (1991). "The Limits of Problem-Based Learning." In *The Challenge of Problem-Based Learning,* edited by D. Boud and G. Feletti. New York: St. Martin's Press.

Duffy, T.M., H. Kremer, and J. Savery. (1994). *Constructivism: Theory and Practice.* Bloomington, Ind.: School of Education, Indiana University.

Fullan, M. (1993). *Change Forces: Probing the Depths of Educational Change.* New York: Falmer Press.

Gallagher, S.A., W.J. Stepien, and H. Rosenthal. (1992). "The Effects of Problem-Based Learning on Problem Solving." *Gifted Child Quarterly* 36, 4: 195–200.

Honebein, P.C., T.M. Duffy, and B.J. Fishman. (1992). "Constructivism and the Design of Learning Environments: Context and Authentic Activities for Learning." In *Designing Environments for Constructive Learning,* edited by T.M. Duffy, J. Lowyck, and D.H. Jonassen. New York: Springer Verlag.

Joyce, B., J. Wolf, and E. Calhoun. (1993). *The Self-Renewing School.* Alexandria, Va.: ASCD.

Lieberman, A. (1988). *Building a Professional Culture in Schools.* New York: Teachers College Press.

Lieberman, A. (1992). "The Meaning of Scholarly Activity and the Building of Community." *Educational Researcher* 21, 6: 5-12.

Lieberman, A. (1996). "Practices That Support Teacher Development: Transforming Conceptions of Professional Learning." In *Teacher Learning: New Policies, New Practices,* edited by M.W. McLaughlin and I. Oberman. New York: Teachers College Press.

Lieberman, A., and L. Miller. (1990). "Restructuring Schools: What Matters Most." *Phi Delta Kappan* 7, 10: 759–764.

Maeroff, G.I. (1993). *Team Building for School Change: Equipping Teachers for New Roles.* New York: Teachers College Press.

Marshall, S. (1993). "Wingspread Conference Report: Problem-Based Learning." Aurora, Ill.: Center for Problem-Based Learning.

Marzano, R.J., R.S. Brandt, C.S. Hughes, B. Fly Jones, B.Z. Presseissen, S.C. Rankin, and C. Suhor. (1988). *Dimensions of Thinking: A Framework for Curriculum and Instruction.* Alexandria, Va.: ASCD.

Matson, J. (1993). "Designing for Failure." In *Teaching Critical Thinking: Reports from Across the Curriculum,* edited by J. Clarke and A. Biddle. Englewood Cliffs, N.J.: Prentice Hall.

McLaughlin, M. (1987). "Learning from Experience: Lessons from Policy Implementation." *Educational Evaluation and Policy Analysis* 9, 2: 171-178.

Newell, A., and H.A. Simon (1972). *Human Problem Solving.* Englewood Cliffs, N.J.: Prentice Hall.

Nickerson, R.S., D.N. Perkins, and E.E. Smith. (1985). *The Teaching of Thinking.* Hillsdale, N.J.: Lawrence Erlbaum Associates.

Norman, G.R., and H.G. Schmidt. (1992). "The Psychological Basis of Problem-Based Learning: A Review of the Evidence." *Academic Medicine* 67, 9: 557–565.

O'Keefe, P., G. Rees, and C. Shepard. (April 4–7, 1992). "The Staff Development Potential of Professional Development Schools: The Transformation of Highland High." Presentation at the 47th Annual Conference of the Association of Supervision and Curriculum Development, New Orleans, La.

Ross, B. (1991). "Towards a Framework for Problem-Based Curricula." In *The Challenge of Problem-Based Learning,* edited by D. Boud and G. Feletti. New York: St. Martin's Press.

Sagor, R. (1992). *How to Conduct Collaborative Action Research.* Alexandria, Va.: ASCD.

Schön, D.A. (1983). *The Reflective Practitioner: How Professionals Think in Action.* New York: Basic Books.

Senge, P.M. (1990). *The Fifth Discipline: The Art and Science of the Learning Organization.* New York: Bantam/Doubleday.

Stepien, W., and S. Gallagher. (1993). "Problem-Based Learning: As Authentic as It Gets. *Educational Leadership* 50, 7: 25–28.

Stepien, W., S. Gallagher, and D. Workman. (1993). "Problem-Based Learning for Traditional and Interdisciplinary Classrooms." Aurora, Ill: Illinois Mathematics and Science Academy. (Draft manuscript available from authors.)

U.S. Department of Education. (1990). *Education Commission of the States Report.* Washington, D.C.: U.S. Government Printing Office.

Wheatley, M. (1992). *Leadership and the New Science: Learning About Organizations from an Orderly Universe.* San Francisco: Berrett-Koehler Publishers, Inc.

Whiting, S. (1988). "What Do Teachers of Adults Need to Know?" ERIC Doc ED324398.

Wildman, J., and J. Niles. (1987). "Essentials of Professional Growth." *Educational Leadership* 44, 5: 4-10.

# ABOUT THE AUTHORS

**Judith A. Aiken** has served as a middle school teacher, guidance counselor, principal, and curriculum director. She began working with Problem-Based School Development teams when she was the Curriculum Coordinator for Union 32 Junior-Senior High School in Montpelier, Vermont. After serving in a number of school leadership positions for many years, she completed her doctorate in curriculum theory and development at Rutgers University. Her extensive experience teaching graduate courses and workshops for educators led her to a full-time faculty position in educational leadership at The University of Vermont. Phone (802) 656-8199. e-mail: jaaiken@zoo.uvm.edu

**John H. Clarke** was an English teacher in Massachusetts and elsewhere before completing a doctorate at Northeastern and moving to The University of Vermont as an instructional developer in 1977. His books include *Patterns of Thinking* (1990); *Teaching Critical Thinking*, with Arthur Biddle (1993); and *Interdisciplinary High School Teaching*, with Russell Agne (1997)—all with Allyn and Bacon in Boston. As coordinator of the secondary education program, he is working to establish Professional Development Schools in Vermont. He may be contacted at The University of Vermont, College of Education and Social Services, Department of Education, Waterman Building, Burlington, VT 05405-0160. Phone: (802) 656-3356. Fax: (802) 656-0004. e-mail: jhclarke@aol.com

**Nancy A. Cornell** was an English teacher in three high schools, a full-time mother, a freelance writer, and a curriculum coordinator in the Rutland Northeast Supervisory District before she took up her present position as Curriculum Coordinator in the Addison Northeast Supervisory District in Bristol, Vermont. Her writing includes many articles on education, childrearing, parenting, and rural life. In Vermont, she has recently become a leader in standards-based curriculum design. Phone: (802) 453-5247. e-mail: ncornell@mtabe.k12.vt.us

**Jane Briody Goodman** is the Foreign Language Department Chair and facilitator of the Freshman Collaborative Program at Essex High School. She has served for five years on the State Professional Standards Board that oversees local teacher licensing and relicensing across the state. Ms. Goodman has been a member of several program approval teams at colleges and universities in Vermont. She earned her MA in French from Middlebury College as well as an MEd from The University of Vermont. Phone: (802) 879-5526. e-mail: jgoodman@ejhs.k12.vp.us

**Karin K. Hess** is an Educational Leader (a member of a three-principal team) at Waterbury-Duxbury School District (preK-8) in Waterbury, Vermont. She is also editor of *Science Exemplars* (a science publication for teaching science assessment) and a member of the design teams developing Vermont's Framework of Standards and Learning Opportunities and the state science assessment. She has authored or coauthored four books on the teaching of writing and many articles on questioning strategies and inquiry science. A former classroom teacher, Ms. Hess has also served as the New Jersey State Director for Gifted Education. She is completing doctoral research in educational reform at The University of Vermont.

**Stephen D. Sanborn** began his career in education teaching both physical education and science using initiative problems, adventure games, and trust activities in wilderness experiences. After 10 years in the classroom, he moved on to assistant principalships at both Colchester Middle School and Essex High School before assuming his present position as Director of Curriculum and Instruction at the Chittenden Central Supervisory Union. He earned his doctorate in Educational Leadership and Policy Studies at The University of Vermont in 1993, where he now teaches courses in curriculum design and staff supervision using a school development/problem-solving model. Steve has worked cooperatively with the university for seven years to create a Professional Development School in Essex Junction. For the past two years he has served as president of Vermont ASCD. Phone: (802) 878-1373. e-mail: ssanborn@ejhs.k12.vt.us